Bloom's Modern Critical Views

Bloom's Modern Critical Views

OSCAR WILDE
New Edition

Edited and with an introduction by
Harold Bloom
Sterling Professor of the Humanities
Yale University

BLOOM'S
LITERARY CRITICISM
An imprint of Infobase Publishing

Bloom's Modern Critical Views: Oscar Wilde—New Edition
Copyright © 2011 by Infobase Publishing
Introduction © 2011 by Harold Bloom

Bloom's Literary Criticism
An imprint of Infobase Publishing
132 West 31st Street
New York NY 10001

Library of Congress Cataloging-in-Publication Data
Oscar Wilde / edited and with an introduction by Harold Bloom. — New ed.
    p. cm. — (Bloom's modern critical interpretations)
    Includes bibliographical references and index.
    ISBN 978-1-60413-881-8 (hardcover)
    1. Wilde, Oscar, 1854–1900—Criticism and interpretation. I. Bloom, Harold.
    II. Title. III. Series.
    PR5824.O82 2010
    828'.809—dc22   2010021316

Contributing editor: Pamela Loos
Cover designed by Takeshi Takahashi
Composition by IBT Global, Troy NY
Cover printed by IBT Global, Troy NY
Book printed and bound by IBT Global, Troy NY
Date printed: November 2010
Printed in the United States of America

10 9 8 7 6 5 4 3 2 1

Contents

Editor's Note

My introduction emphasizes that Wilde's rightness as a critic is central to his achievement as a writer.

Wilde's most distinguished scholar, the biographer Richard Ellmann, opens the volume with a discussion of decadent aestheticism in Wilde and his immediate successors.

Guy Willoughby then examines how Wilde's imaginative writings anticipate the transformed aesthetic views on display in *De Profundis*.

Ronald Knowles traces the carnivalesque elements found in Wilde's acknowledged masterpiece, *The Importance of Being Earnest*, after which Michael Patrick Gillespie considers the combination of familiarity and innovation that informs Wilde's signature comedy.

John Paul Riquelme detects the shadow of Pater in *The Picture of Dorian Gray*, followed by Christopher S. Nassaar's reading of *Salomé*.

Burkhard Niederhoff returns to *Earnest* and its interweaving of parody and paradox, and James G. Nelson concludes the volume with an analysis of the romantic overtones informing Wilde's body of work.

HAROLD BLOOM

Introduction

Oscar Wilde first published a book in 1881, and after more than 125 years, literary opinion has converged in the judgment that Wilde, as Borges asserts, was almost always right. This rightness, which transcends wit, is now seen as central to the importance of being Oscar. Daily my mail brings me bad poetry, printed and unprinted, and daily I murmur to myself Wilde's apothegm: "All bad poetry springs from genuine feeling." Arthur Symons, like Wilde a disciple of Walter Pater, reviewed the Paterian *Intentions* of Wilde with this exquisite summary: "He is conscious of the charm of graceful echoes, and is always original in his quotations." Symons understood that Wilde, even as playwright and as storyteller, was essentially a critic, just as Pater's fictions were primarily criticism.

Wilde began as a poet and alas was and always remained quite a bad poet. An admirer of *The Ballad of Reading Gaol* should read the poem side by side with *The Ancient Mariner*, in order to see precisely its crippling failure to experience an anxiety of influence. Of course, Ruskin and Pater also began as poets but then wisely gave it up almost immediately, unlike Matthew Arnold who waited a little too long. It is deeply unfortunate that the young Wilde gave the world this poem about Mazzini:

> He is not dead, the immemorial Fates
> Forbid it, and the closing shears refrain,
> Lift up your heads, ye everlasting gates!
> Ye argent clarions sound a loftier strain!

1

For the vile thing he hated lurks within
Its sombre house, alone with God and memories of sin.

This dreadful travesty and amalgam of Shelley, Swinburne, the Bible, Milton, and whatnot is typical of Wilde's verse and opened him to many attacks that became particularly nasty in America during his notorious lecture tour of 1882. Thomas Wentworth Higginson, whom we remember as Emily Dickinson's amiable and uncomprehending "Mentor," made a public attack on Wilde's poetic immorality that expanded into an accusation of cowardice for not taking part in the Irish national struggle: "Is it manhood for her gifted sons to stay at home and help work out the problem; or to cross the Atlantic and pose in ladies' boudoirs or write prurient poems which their hostesses must discreetly ignore?" The force of Higginson's rhetoric evaporates for us when we remember that the burly Wilde was no coward, physical or moral, and also when we remember that Higginson, with his customary blindness, linked Wilde to Walt Whitman's work as a wound dresser in the Washington, D.C., Civil War hospitals: "I am one of many to whom Whitman's 'Drum-Taps' have always sounded as hollow as the instrument they counterfeit." Why, Higginson demanded, had not Whitman's admirable physique gone into battle with the Union armies? A Civil War hero himself, Higginson would have had no scruples about hurling the middle-aged bard and idler into battle. We can credit W. B. Yeats with more insight into Wilde, let alone into Whitman, than Higginson displayed, since Yeats insisted that Wilde was essentially a man of action displaced into a man of letters. In some curious sense, there is a sickness-unto-action in Wilde's life and work, a masked despair that led him to the borders of that realm of fantasy the Victorians called "nonsense" literature, the cosmos of Edward Lear. Lionel Trilling aptly located Wilde's masterpiece, *The Importance of Being Earnest*, in that world, and it seems to me never far from Wilde's work. The metaphysical despair of ever knowing or speaking truth Wilde probably absorbed from his nearest precursor, Walter Pater, whose "Sebastian Van Storck" in *Imaginary Portraits* is a major depiction of intellectual despair. Wilde, deliberately less subtle than his evasive master, Pater, speaks out directly through his mouthpiece, Algernon, in the original, four-act version of *The Importance of Being Earnest*:

My experience of life is that whenever one tells a lie one is corroborated on every side. When one tells the truth one is left in a very lonely and painful position, and no one believes a word one says.

Wilde's most profound single work is "The Decay of Lying: An Observation," an essay in what now would be called literary theory brilliantly cast in dialogue form. Vivian, speaking for Wilde, rejects what passes for lying in mere politicians:

> They never rise beyond the level of misrepresentation, and actually condescend to prove, to discuss, to argue. How different from the temper of the true liar, with his frank, fearless statements, his superb irresponsibility, his healthy, natural disdain of proof of any kind! After all, what is a fine lie? Simply that which is its own evidence. If a man is sufficiently unimaginative to produce evidence in support of a lie, he might just as well speak the truth at once.

Lying, then, is opposed to misrepresentation, because aesthetic lying is a kind of supermimesis and is set, not against truth or reality, but against time and antithetically against time's slave, nature. As Vivian remarks: "Nothing is more evident than that Nature Hates Mind. Thinking is the most unhealthy thing in the world, and people die of it just as they die of any other disease. Fortunately, in England at any rate, thought is not catching." Nature's redemption can come only through imitating art. We can believe that Wilde's deathbed conversion to the Church was simply a reaffirmation of his lifelong belief that Christ was an artist, not in Wilde a frivolous belief but a heretical one, indeed an aesthetic version of Gnosticism. Hence Wilde's preference for the fourth Gospel, which he shrewdly regarded as Gnostic:

> While in reading the Gospels—particularly that of St. John himself, or whatever early Gnostic took his name and mantle—I see the continual assertion of the imagination as the basis of all spiritual and material life, I see also that to Christ imagination was simply a form of love, and that to him love was lord in the fullest meaning of the phrase.

This is Wilde speaking out of the depths, in *De Profundis*, the epistle addressed to Lord Alfred Douglas from Reading Gaol. G. Wilson Knight, startlingly linking Wilde and Christ, hints that the ideology of Wilde's homosexuality was its dominant element, involving the raising of love to the high realm of aesthetic contemplation. Without disputing Knight (or Wilde), one can observe that such an elevation is more like Pater than Plato, more like the lying against time that is the privileged moment than the lying against mortality that is the realm of the timeless ideas. As Pater's most dangerous disciple, Wilde literalizes Pater's valorization of perception over nature, of impression over description.

Wilde stands between Pater and Yeats, between a doctrine of momentary aesthetic ecstasies, phantasmagoric hard gemlike flames, and a vision of lyric simplification through aesthetic intensity, what Yeats called the condition of fire. Pater, and not Lord Alfred Douglas, was Wilde's disaster, as Yeats knew and intimated. Though his immediate sources were in Ruskin, Swinburne, and the Pre-Raphaelites, Pater's sensibility went back to the Keats of the "Ode on Melancholy." Wilde, High Romantic in every way, nevertheless did not have a romantic sensibility, which is why his verse, derived from all of the romantics, is so hopelessly inadequate. As a sensibility, Wilde is a fantastic version of Congreve and Sheridan and Goldsmith; an Anglo-Irish wit wandering in the regions of Lewis Carroll, W. S. Gilbert, and Edward Lear, to repeat Trilling's insight again. Nonsense is the truest rejection of mere nature and the strongest program for compelling nature to cease imitating itself and to imitate art instead. Wilde's theory of criticism achieves magnificence when it extravagantly leaps over sense into the cognitive phantasmagoria of a true theory of the lie, an escape from time into the fantasy of interpretation:

> I know that you are fond of Japanese things. Now, do you really imagine that the Japanese people, as they are presented to us in art, have any existence? If you do, you have never understood Japanese art at all. The Japanese people are the deliberate selfconscious creation of certain individual artists. If you set a picture by Hokusai, or Hokkei, or any of the great native painters, beside a real Japanese gentleman or lady, you will see that there is not the slightest resemblance between them. The actual people who live in Japan are not unlike the general run of English people; that is to say, they are extremely commonplace, and have nothing extraordinary or curious about them. In fact the whole of Japan is a pure invention. There is no such country, there are no such people. One of our most charming painters went recently to the Land of the Chrysanthemum in the foolish hope of seeing the Japanese. All he saw, all he had a chance of painting, were a few lanterns and some fans.

In fact the whole of Japan is a pure invention. There is no such country, there are no such people. That is certainly one of the grand critical epiphanies, one of those privileged moments that alone make criticism memorable. Japan momentarily becomes one with that far and wide land where the Jumblies live, where the Pobble who has no toes and the Dong with a luminous nose dwell together. It is also the land of the Canon Chasuble and Miss Prism and

Lady Bracknell, the land of cucumber sandwiches where Wilde deserved and desired to live. Call it, surprisingly enough, what Wilde called it, the land of the highest criticism:

> ... I would say that the highest Criticism, being the purest form of personal impression, is in its way more creative than creation, as it has least reference to any standard external to itself, and is, in fact, its own reason for existing, and, as the Greeks would put it, in itself, and to itself, an end. Certainly, it is never trammelled by any shackles of verisimilitude. No ignoble considerations of probability, that cowardly concession to the tedious repetitions of domestic or public life, affect it ever. One may appeal from fiction unto fact. But from the soul there is no appeal.

Call this Wilde's credo, or as Richard Ellmann, his crucial scholar, words it, "The Critic as Artist as Wilde." It leads to an even finer declaration, which catches the whole movement from Ruskin and Pater through Wilde and on to Yeats and Wallace Stevens in their critical essays:

> That is what the highest criticism really is, the record of one's own soul. It is more fascinating than history, as it is concerned simply with oneself. It is more delightful than philosophy, as its subject is concrete and not abstract, real and not vague. It is the only civilized form of autobiography, as it deals not with the events, but with the thoughts of one's life; not with life's physical accidents of deed or circumstance, but with the spiritual moods and imaginative passions of the mind.

The only civilized form of autobiography: I know of no better description of authentic criticism. What we want from a critic is not ideology and not method, not philosophy and not history, not theology and not linguistics, not semiotics and not technique, not feminism and not sociology, but precisely the moods and passions of cognition, of imagining, of the life of the spirit. If you want Marx and Hegel, Heidegger and Lacan and their revisionists, then take them, but if you want literary criticism, then turn to Hazlitt and Ruskin, to Pater and Wilde. Wilde's unique gift is the mode of wit by which he warns us against falling into careless habits of accuracy and by which he instructs us that the primary aim of the critic is to see the object as in itself it really is not.

Why then did Wilde rush to social destruction? On February 14, 1895, *The Importance of Being Earnest* opened in London, only six weeks after the opening of *An Ideal Husband*. Wilde was 41, in the full possession of his talents and his health. On February 28, he found the Marquis of Queensberry's card waiting for him at the Albemarle Club, with its illiterate, nasty address "To Oscar Wilde, posing as a somdomite [*sic*]," in which the weird touch of "posing" failed to amuse him. His note of that day to his close friend Robert Ross has an uncharacteristic tone of hysteria:

> Bosie's father has left a card at my club with hideous words on it. I don't see anything now but a criminal prosecution. My whole life seems ruined by this man. The tower of ivory is assailed by the foul thing. On the sand is my life spilt. I don't know what to do.

Had he done nothing he would not have found himself, less than three months later, sentenced to two years' hard labor. Richard Ellmann speaks of Wilde's "usual cycle which ran from scapegrace to scapegoat." Whatever its psychopathology, or even its psychopoetics, its most salient quality seems to be a vertigo-inducing speed. Freud presumably would have found in it the economics of moral masochism, the need for punishment. Yeats subtly interpreted it as due to the frustrations of a man who should have spent himself in action, military or political. One remembers Lady Bracknell remarking of Jack's and Algernon's father that, "The General was essentially a man of peace, except in his domestic life," an observation that perhaps precludes any vision of Wilde in battle or in political strife. The economic problem of masochism doubtless had its place within Wilde, but few moralists hated pain more than Wilde, and nothing even in Wilde surpasses the moral beauty of the closing pages of "The Soul of Man under Socialism":

> Pain is not the ultimate mode of perfection. It is merely provisional and a protest. It has reference to wrong, unhealthy, unjust surroundings. When the wrong, and the disease, and the injustice are removed, it will have no further place. It will have done its work. It was a great work, but it is almost over. Its sphere lessens every day.
>   *Nor will man miss it. For what man has sought for is, indeed, neither pain nor pleasure, but simply Life.* [Wilde's italics]

We remember, reading this, that Wilde was Ruskin's disciple as well as Pater's. Ruskin's credo, as phrased in *Unto This Last*, is the prophetic basis for Wilde's social vision:

There is no wealth but Life—Life, including all its powers of love, of joy, and of admiration. That country is the richest which nourishes the greatest number of noble and happy human beings.

Why then was the author of "The Soul of Man under Socialism" and of *The Importance of Being Earnest* so doom eager? His best poem was not in verse but is the extraordinary prose poem of 1893, "The Disciple":

> When Narcissus died the pool of his pleasure changed from a cup of sweet waters into a cup of salt tears, and the Oreads came weeping through the woodland that they might sing to the pool and give it comfort.
>
> And when they saw that the pool had changed from a cup of sweet waters into a cup of salt tears, they loosened the green tresses of their hair and cried to the pool and said, 'We do not wonder that you should mourn in this manner for Narcissus, so beautiful was he.'
>
> 'But was Narcissus beautiful?' said the pool.
>
> 'Who should know better than you?' answered the Oreads. 'Us did he ever pass by, but you he sought for, and would lie on your banks and look down at you, and in the mirror of your waters he would mirror his own beauty.'
>
> And the pool answered, 'But I loved Narcissus because, as he lay on my banks and looked down at me, in the mirror of his eyes I saw ever my own beauty mirrored.'

Kierkegaard might have called this "The Case of the Contemporary Disciple Doubled." Narcissus never saw the pool, nor the pool Narcissus, but at least the pool mourns him. Wilde's despair transcended even his humane wit and could not be healed by the critical spirit or by the marvelous rightness of his perceptions and sensations.

The Importance of Being Earnest

I recall writing that, in Lady Augusta Bracknell's rolling periods, Oscar Wilde fused the rhetorical prose styles of Dr. Samuel Johnson and Shakespeare's Sir John Falstaff. "Rise, sir, from this semirecumbent posture. It is most indecorous" competes with "Human life is everywhere a condition where much is to be endured and little to be enjoyed." And again with "O thou hast damnable iteration and art indeed able to corrupt a saint. Thou hast done much harm upon me, Hal, God forgive you for it! Before I knew thee, Hal, I knew nothing and now to speak truly am I become little better than one of the wicked." Falstaff is the most elaborate, Johnson the most severe, Bracknell the most outrageous, but all are outrageous enough, and none accepts any demurral.

From her first entrance, Lady Bracknell is on the attack, a dreadnought firing from all turrets:

> Good afternoon, dear Algernon, I hope you are behaving quite well.

She proceeds to disapprove, massively, of the mythical invalid, Bunbury, Algernon's excuse for getting away on country junkets:

> Well, I must say, Algernon, that I think it is high time that Mr. Bunbury made up his mind whether he was going to live or die. This shilly-shallying with the question is absurd.

In some respects, Lady Augusta Bracknell is an ironic prophecy of the Conservative prime minister Dame Margaret Thatcher, iron field marshal of the British victory over the Argentines in the Falklands War. One can see Lady Bracknell in the role, perhaps with Groucho Marx as her adjutant, since heroic farce is her mode. The finest Lady Bracknell I have seen is Dame Edith Evans, in the splendid Anthony Asquith film that features also Michael Redgrave and Margaret Rutherford. Dame Edith played the role as it must be performed, with Wagnerian severity and frowning high seriousness.

Lady Bracknell, a sublime monster, in some respects is larger than the play, just as the dread Juno is too gigantic a menace even for the *Aeneid*. When I think of Oscar Wilde's work, I always first recall *Earnest* and then cheer myself up by rolling forth various grand pronouncements of the magnificent Augusta. Wilde said of his greatest play: "It is written by a butterfly for butterflies," which is also very cheering. If Lady Bracknell, in full flight, is a butterfly, then we are listening to an iron butterfly:

> To lose one parent, Mr. Worthing, may be regarded as a misfortune; to lose both looks like carelessness. I dislike arguments of any kind. They are always vulgar, and often convincing. The General was essentially a man of peace, except in his domestic life.

Lady Bracknell's is the voice of authority, that is to say of social authority and, therefore, madness. Her lunacy is founded on a solipsism so absolute as to be very nearly without rival:

Come, dear, we have already missed five, if not six, trains. To miss
any more might expose us to comment on the platform.

I join my friend Camille Paglia in my passion for this truly gorgeous expression of solipsism. Lady Bracknell's greatness is that she would not comprehend that no one on the platform possibly could know how many trains she had missed, since she cannot conceive of her absence but only of her overwhelming presence.

RICHARD ELLMANN

The Uses of Decadence: Wilde, Yeats and Joyce

Victorian melancholy disclosed its uneasiness in the concept of decadence. The word began to be used in England about 1850, as if the distentions of empire necessarily entailed spiritual decline and fall. "Decadent" was not a word that Ruskin or Arnold found congenial: Ruskin preferred "corruption" and Arnold "philistinism" and "barbarism." But decadence, with implications of the fading day, season and century, had an unfamiliar ring and gradually came to seem the right word. As if to confirm its rightness, the principal guardians of the Victorian age in statecraft and in literature ailed and then died symbolically as well as literally. Most were gone by the time the nineties started. "The woods decay, the woods decay and fall."

What distinguished decadence from corruption or philistinism was that it could be discussed with relish as well as with concern. Gautier, whose writings were in vogue in England as well as in France, declared in his preface to Baudelaire's *Les fleurs du mal* in 1868 that the decadent spirit was in harmony with the contemporary crisis. He interpreted decadence as the extreme point of maturity of a civilisation. Paul Verlaine could accordingly announce in 1883 with *Schadenfreude* rather than discomfiture, "Je suis l'Empire à la fin de la Décadence." Dying cultures make the best cultures. A few months after Verlaine's poem came Huysmans's novel *À Rebours*, to give decadence the force of a programme. His decadent nobleman (decadents are always male

From *Literary Interrelations: Ireland, England and the World*, edited by Wolfgang Zach and Heinz Kosok, pp. 27–39. Copyright © 1987 by Gunter Narr Verlag Tübingen.

11

and preferably noble; female decadents are called by other names) has no normal tastes. A determined quester for unheard-of pleasures, he collapses at last in neurasthenia, but of the most glamorous kind. This powerful work outlasted all other decadent prose because it established a new type—the sampler, who keeps changing his drink, who moves from one inordinate and esoteric fancy to another. *À Rebours* became at once a favourite book of Whistler, Wilde, George Moore, Arthur Symons. Wilde and Moore wrote books that in part derived from it, and something of the book's effect rubbed off on Wilde's life as well. The cult of the green carnation, for instance, probably stemmed from Des Esseintes's peculiar notion that, while artificial flowers were to be preferred to natural ones, best of all would be natural flowers that looked like artificial ones. (A florist in the Burlington Arcade painted white carnations green every day.) What was also valuable about *À Rebours* was that it criticized decadence even while touting it. The intricate schemes of Des Esseintes to amuse himself with new sensations are checked as much by Huysmans's sardonic irony as by their inherent futility, and Huysmans, while never indifferent to his hero, avoids identification with him.

À Rebours was read with more solemnity than it was written with, and remained for a time the bible of decadence. Devotees of that movement were as determined in their advocacy as its bourgeois adversaries in their rejection. They flourished, however, for only a few years in Paris, during the eighties. By the time English writers took an interest in decadence it had already lost its lustre, or what they labelled (in a mistranslation of Baudelaire) "its phosphorescence of putrescence." In England nobody called himself a decadent, though it was a fine epithet to ascribe to someone else. Ten years after Verlaine's poem Arthur Symons published his article in *Harper's* on "The Decadent Movement in Literature." Symons expressed a wry fondness for decadence as "a new and interesting and beautiful disease," but within a few years he acknowledged that the decadent movement had been "an interlude, a half-mock interlude." He was persuaded later to call the movement "symbolist" rather than decadent, a change of title which had already taken place in Paris ten years earlier. The element of mockery was overt in Oscar Wilde's references to decadence in the late 1880s. He spoke of a new club called "The Tired Hedonists" who, he said, "wore faded roses in their buttonholes" and "had a sort of cult for Domitian." The essay in which he evoked this fantasy movement was "The Decay of Lying," the title itself a mockery of decadence.

The fact that in England decadence never gained the status of a literary movement did not keep people from taking sides about it. It was a subject of debate, it affected the course of literature, it did everything but exist. What opponents of decadence meant by the word was principally its parent movement, aestheticism. The battle lines had been drawn early in the century in two books. One was Gautier's *Mademoiselle de Maupin* (1837), the other Kierkegaard's *Either/Or* (1843). Gautier provided a heroine with bisexual tastes; in his preface he scorned morality, social utility, and nature as points of reference for art. Art was amoral, useless, and unnatural. Kierkegaard took up aesthetic man, as opposed to ethical man, and anatomised the way in which aesthetic man sought to be absorbed in a mood, a mood which must necessarily be only a fragment of himself. For fear of losing the mood, he cannot afford to reflect, nor can he attempt to be more than what he for that mood-moment is. He moves from sensation to sensation, much in the manner that Pater was later to extol; Kierkegaard seems to be refuting Pater before Pater wrote.

During the century both aestheticism and anti-aestheticism gathered force. In Joyce's *Stephen Hero* the president of the college warns Stephen, "Estheticism often begins well but ends in the vilest abominations...." The term could still be used without reproach, however. In 1868 Pater described the Pre-Raphaelites under the honorific title of the "aesthetic movement." But the counter-movement had its weapons of ridicule. In 1881 Gilbert's *Patience* presented an aesthete—Bunthorne—as effeminate and narcissistic. Up to now no memorable type of decadent aestheticism had been evolved in English literature to match Huysmans's character Des Esseintes, but Pater tried to establish one with his *Marius the Epicurean*, published two years after *À Rebours*. Marius is also a sampler, attracted to a series of cults like a series of sensations; one of them is a new Cyrenaicism, which, as Pater explains, "from time to time breaks beyond the limits of the actual moral order, perhaps not without some pleasurable excitement in so bold a venture." As his double negative indicates, Pater was a cautious man. His Marius is cautious too, and cannot be said to succumb to Cyrenaicism or to Christianity either; he seeks the impassioned realisation of experience, but in so sober-sided a way as to deprive aestheticism of its unwholesomeness. (For true decadent aestheticism a gamy whiff of the Borgias is required.) Pater situated his story in imperial Rome during the reign of Marcus Aurelius, and so left it open for someone else to provide a more modern and English instance. This was exactly what Wilde tried to furnish in *The Picture of Dorian Gray*, first published four years after *Marius* and part of the same cycle of novels.

The familiar ways of attacking decadent aestheticism were to quarrel with its supposed morbidity and pretentiousness, its narcissism, its excesses in technique and language, its concern with mere sensation, its artificiality and abnormality. Most of these criticisms could easily be turned against those who made them. Wilde said that, if one looked for examples of decay, one would find them among the sincere, the honest, the earnest. In *Ecce Homo*

Nietzsche declares, "Agreed that I am a decadent, I am also the reverse." By his lights "morality itself" was "a symptom of decadence." It was a revenge upon life, an attempt to "unself man" (*Ecce Homo*). In *Stephen Hero* Joyce acknowledged that at moments Stephen showed signs of decadence, then added, "But we cannot but see a process to life through corruption." One man's decadence was another man's renaissance. Mallarmé saw in the dying century "the fluttering of the veil of the temple," as if some infinite revelation were in store ("Crise des vers"). So Yeats wrote an essay under the title "The Autumn of the Flesh" in 1896, and said, in ninetyish rhythm, "I see, indeed, in the arts of every country those faint lights and faint colours and faint outlines and faint energies which many call "the decadence" and which I, because I believe that the arts lie dreaming of things to come, prefer to call the autumn of the flesh." The best season is autumn, and the best time of day is of course the Celtic twilight, which also heralded a victory of moonlit spirit over sunlit matter. Wilde, less mystically, offered the heraldic figure of the new man, the *do-nothing*, a creature who emerges only after five in the afternoon, what used to be called "the lounge lizard." In a period when Victorians were infernally busy in misdoing everything, what really needed to be recognized was what he called "the importance of doing absolutely nothing." Under cover of indolence, which others were free to call decadence if they liked, Wilde proposed to transform society.

The debate about decadence achieved such resonance that any account of the nineties must take notice of it. C. E. M. Bowra reports in his *Memoirs* that Yeats wrote to him, "The 'nineties was in reality a period of very great vigour, thought and passion were breaking free from tradition." The allegation that they were decaying prompted writers to disprove the charge. In so doing, they had to rethink problems of art, language, nature, life, religion, myth. Wilde is the supreme example. He had adopted aestheticism while still at Trinity College, Dublin, and in the early 1880s he went to America to present the doctrine under the title of the English renaissance. At the time he was between two versions of aestheticism. One, deriving from Gautier, and supported by Whistler, extolled art for its absolute uselessness and its elitism, and denied that it had any but a perfunctory connection with life and nature. The other held that art could remake the world. In America Wilde spent most of his time extolling beauty, but he also urged that artistic principles might beautify houses and dress as well as life generally. This meant that it was not useless, nor necessarily elitist.

Wilde preached renaissance for a whole year to the Americans, then returned and went to Paris. He found himself there *en pleine décadence*. Parisian decadence made his inveterate proselytising for undefined beauty seem somewhat out of date. Soon after returning to England, Wilde made clear in a review that he did not at all accept that art was for art's sake. That slogan referred only to what the artist feels when he is composing, and had nothing to do with the general motive of art. Towards the end of the eighties Wilde propounded such a general motive of art in "The Decay of Lying." In this he turned Aristotle on his head by saying that art does not imitate nature, nature imitates art. It was a paradox that no one had been able to state so succinctly before, though it had certainly been implied by the Romantics. The effect was not to divorce art from life, as Whistler and Gautier would do, but to bring the two together again, though with the priorities changed. The difference between Wilde and the Romantics was not in estimating the value of art, but in putting so much emphasis as Wilde did on artifice. When he said, "A sunset is no doubt a beautiful thing, but perhaps its chief use is to illustrate quotations from the poets," he was suggesting that artists were not only the Shelleyan unacknowledged legislators, but the quickeners of perception. Nature as we know it is built up out of imaginative fictions. Strip as we will, we will never be naked. People fall in love because poets have talked up that sentiment. They limp because Byron limped, they dress up because Beau Brummel did, Wilde's point here being that people are affected not only by the works of art that are written down, but by the works of art that are lived. This view of art was not at all elitist; it was democratic and inescapable. Wilde set himself against the contempt that Whistler expressed for art critics, which derived from Gautier's comment, "There was no art criticism under Julius II." Wilde's contrary view was, "The Greeks were a nation of art critics," and he would have said the same of the Italians of the Renaissance. For criticism was one way in which expression could recognize its cultural antecedents. In his other great essay, "The Critic as Artist," he explained that if it were not for criticism art would merely repeat itself. But, since all fine imaginative work is self-conscious and deliberate, the role of criticism is to subvert what has just been done, by confronting it with what was done before and elsewhere. The critical faculty brings to bear "the concentrated experience of the race" as opposed to momentary consolidations arrived at by individual artists. Art is a great subverter, but always in danger of forgetting to subvert. Criticism prevents art from forgetting, prevents it from sinking into conformity. The image of subversion leads Wilde to see the artist and the critic within the artist as in some sense criminal. He disrupts, he destroys as he creates. In pursuing ever ampler and as yet unaccepted versions of the world, the artist is always breaking bonds.

The effect is to challenge all effigies, all that is established, such as the established virtues. Chastity is a virtue for which, as Renan says, nature cares little, and art, according to Wilde, correspondingly little. Charity creates a false sense of obligation, since the rich have no right to their wealth any more than the poor to their poverty. As for self-sacrifice, Wilde says that only a thoroughly secular age such as our own deifies it, for self-sacrifice is a survival of the self-mutilation of the savage and part of the old worship of pain. (This was not his final word on the subject.) It involves exactly that contraction of impulse, that narrowing in, which art sets itself to overcome. Wilde examines, or rather cross-examines, all the accepted virtues. So he takes up the virtue of presence of mind. He had a story to illustrate this. Once, in a crowded theatre, the audience saw smoke rising from the wings. They panicked and ran for the exits. But a leading actor, a man with presence of mind, went to the prosce-nium and called out, "Ladies and Gentlemen, there is nothing to worry about. This tiny disturbance is of no consequence. The real danger to you is your own panic. The best thing for you to do is to go back to your seats." They all turned and went back to their seats, and . . . were burned to a crisp.

The virtues are all to be tested afresh, then, and in fact all things require testing. The artist, equipped with a critical eye that constantly enforces a larger context—as, for example, of Greece and Rome as well as Christianity, has this task to perform. We speak of the artistic imagination, but what we mean is this eye for "the concentrated experience of the race" which keeps the new from solidifying. Writ large, this shift in perception brings a new dispensation—Wilde speaks of it as the "new Hellenism" as in youth he had spoken of it as the Renaissance. Does it matter whether we call it decadent or resurgent? He thinks not, and simply says, "When that day dawns, or sunset reddens," as if either phrase would do so long as we recognise that the world will be changed.

Without having read Nietzsche, Wilde had arrived at something of the same view of things. In their different ways, both were constructing a new man, what Wallace Stevens called a "major man." Wilde did not share Nietzsche's elaborate view of the genealogy of morals, by which Christianity overturned the pagan virtues and put a morality of slavery in their places; but he did see hypocrisy all about him, masquerading as seriousness. His concep-tion of the major man was of the artist who dared to "harrow the house of the dead." Nietzsche would have agreed.

In making the artist an advance man rather than a camp-follower of his society, Wilde implied that the artist is by necessity as well as choice a deviant. His sense of his own sexual deviation helped him to find justifica-tion for this view. (Later writers such as D. H. Lawrence also made an alli-ance between their sexual and their artistic needs.) In Wilde's time the word "homosexual" was not in use, but there was no less need to find warrant for what it signified. Wilde became the first writer in English since Christopher Marlowe to make a case for it in public. One of his ways of doing so is to attack homosexuality's enemies: the puritans. He does so in his plays in the nineties as he demonstrates, in one play after another, that moral questions are too complex to be solved by puritan mottoes. He never defended homosexuality overtly, except once at his trial, and the present generation, happily uncloseted, are sometimes indignant with him for not having made himself more convincingly and openly the victim of society, the first "Homintern martyr" (in Auden's phrase). I think Wilde felt he could be more effective by opening a window here and there than by seeking martyrdom through taking off the roof, and, given the age in which he lived, that monstrous age, who can say that he was wrong? He saw himself as a rebel, not as a missionary. Homosexuality was not a cause; it was a way of affronting complacency. In three works, between 1889 and 1892, Wilde therefore outraged heterosexual smugness.

The first was *The Portrait of Mr. W. H.*, which played with the idea that Shakespeare was a homosexual, and that he wrote the sonnets to his "dearmylove," Mr. W. H. He does not actually endorse the view, but he disseminates it. Wilde had begun his perilous campaign to bring this forbidden theme into literature by reconstructing the image of Shakespeare himself. He continued this campaign in *The Picture of Dorian Gray*. Dorian not only espouses decadence; he decays in every way except physically, the physical decay being consigned till the book's end to his portrait. He is driven to ruin men and women alike, as if his love in either mode were genuine only to the extent that it is tainted. As in *A Rebours* or, for that matter, in *The Waste Land*, a later decadence, both forms of love are introduced as equally corrupt. Wilde did not celebrate homosexuality, but, then, neither did Proust. In both writers, this deviation is described in terms of unhappiness. But to mention it at all in a society which pretended it did not exist was courageous, and for Wilde, as events proved, foolhardy. The book is also a criticism of the aesthete type, who samples sins and regrets it. Dorian lacks the motive of art, has only its artificializing mechanism. He enslaves instead of emancipating himself. We almost forgive him because he is so beautiful. In *Salomé* the pageboy loves the Syrian soldier, but this is only one of the erotic relationships suggested. For the Syrian, like Herod, loves Salomé; Salomé loves John the Baptist; John the Baptist loves Jesus. All love appears as deviation, and no deviation is superior to any other. All bring their tragic consequences. Wilde improves upon the Bible also by making Iokanaan as hysterical in hatred as Salomé is hysterical in love, so that the reader feels about the same concern for his being decapitated and for her being smothered. Originally Wilde intended to have both of them decapitated as if to confirm their parity. Wilde said elsewhere that renunciation, like excess, brings its own punishment, chastity being just as tendentious as debauchery. Mario Praz finds that the play exhibits the *femme fatale* in all her cruelty, but it seems to exhibit rather the uncontrollability of passion. Though Praz claims it is all plagiarised, and is baffled by its surviving better than other versions, the reason is simple—only Wilde's *Salomé* reconstitutes the entire legend, St John as well as Salomé, and in terms of a strong and original attitude.

With these writings Wilde stretched the domain of literature: he suggested that art might deal critically with moral taboos as part of an effort to remake the world. As Herbert Marcuse says, art shatters everyday experiences and anticipates a different reality principle. Wilde did for English literature almost singlehandedly what a score of writers in France had been attempting for a dozen years. The result was soon apparent. A. E. Housman was empowered to write, in the year of Wilde's trial, *A Shropshire Lad*, with its thinly veiled interest in boys; he sent it to Wilde as he was being released from prison. The next year Rhoda Broughton, who did not like Wilde but was quick to sense the way the wind was blowing, wrote her novel *Faustina*, which is the first lesbian novel in English. Even Henry James wrote a series of works which took advantage of the freedom that Wilde had won for art even while losing his own freedom. Among them perhaps the most important for my purpose is *The Turn of the Screw* (1897), in which James indicates that boy and valet, and girl and governess, pair off for long hours together, and that the boy is expelled from school for some unnamable act of corruption of his schoolmates, which is described as being "against nature." Of course his offence is never specified. By presenting, even if with deliberate vagueness, homosexuality in terms of the corruption of children by adults, James follows Wilde's lead in broaching the subject, and he too associates it with bad conduct, though he too was inclined that way. It is in large part thanks to Wilde, then, both to his books and to his trial testimony, that the taboo against writing about homosexual behaviour or other forms of sexuality begins to be lifted in England. Opening our eyes has been the principal labour of modern literature.

In only one of his works did Wilde attempt to say what the renaissance would be like. That is *The Soul of Man under Socialism*. It would be a time when art would be triumphant, when people would develop freely, when there would be a new Hellenism devoid of the slavery that marked the old Hellenism, when nobody would have to be concerned about the poor, because there would be no poor, nobody would fight for property, because there would be none, nobody would marry, because marriage, being merely an extension of property, would also be abolished. In his letter to Douglas, *De Profundis*, Wilde imagined in muted terms that Christ, whom he now accepted at last, but as the supreme aesthete, would bring about a renaissance by being recognized as a model—for Christ created himself, out of his own imagination, and asserted the imagination as the basis of all spiritual and material life. There are no laws, only exceptions. Sin and suffering were for him modes of perfection. So Wilde found place for suffering, at last, as leading to reconstitution of the terms of existence.

Yeats was in many ways a disciple of Wilde. When he was eighteen he heard Wilde give a lecture in Dublin, and when he was twenty-two he met Wilde at the home of William Ernest Henley. This was the famous occasion when Wilde praised Pater's book on the Renaissance—"It is my golden book. I never travel anywhere without it, but it is the very flower of decadence; the last trumpet should have sounded the moment it was written." "But," someone interjected, "would you not have given us time to read it?" "Oh, no," said Wilde, "there would have been plenty of time afterwards, in either world." Wilde was praising Pater for his decadence, and also suggesting that Pater's readers might as likely go to hell as to heaven. He recognized the ambiguity of Pater's morality. But the decisive moment in the early relationship of Wilde and Yeats came after the Christmas dinner at Wilde's to which Yeats was invited in 1888, when he was twenty-three. At 16 Tite Street he saw the extraordinary decor—drawing-room and dining-room done in white, not only walls but furniture and rugs too, the only exception being the red lampshade suspended from the ceiling. This cowled a terra cotta statue which stood on a diamond-shaped cloth in the middle of a white table. After dinner Wilde brought out the proofs of his essay "The Decay of Lying," and read it to Yeats. It had a profound effect. Yeats was quite prepared to believe that lies were better than truth, for he had already written in "The Song of the Happy Shepherd,"

> The woods of Arcady are dead,
> And over is their antique joy;
> Of old the world on dreaming fed;
> Grey Truth is now her painted toy.

He would say this more vigorously in his verse dialogue "Ego Dominus Tuus," where the first of the two speakers, Hic, pleads for sincerity and veracity so that one can be what one really is, and the second, Ille, pleads for masks and images to enable one to be more than one really is. Ille of course wins. In his edition of Blake, Yeats redefined truth in the light of aestheticism: it is "the dramatic expression of the most complete man." Pater and Wilde would have approved.

Much of "The Decay of Lying" deals with the value of images in shaping our awareness of the world. Wilde insists, for example, that "the whole of Japan is a pure invention. There is no such country, there are no such people." It is a concoction of the artists, to which they have given the name "Japan." Yeats would do something similar with Byzantium, which in his poems must be taken as a pure invention also. It bears no resemblance to the historical Constantinople, but is a city of imagination made by its artists, a magnificent "instead" conjured up by an aging Irishman seeking an antidote for his own time. In his first poem on the subject, Yeats made the city somewhat static, and he wrote a second poem to give it the dynamism that he, like Wilde, regarded as essential to avoid art's repeating itself.

Although Yeats in the nineties scouted the idea of literary decadence, he wrote many poems about the decadence of the modern world. When he says in "The Second Coming," "Things fall apart, the centre cannot hold, / Mere anarchy is loosed upon the world," he has at least the satisfaction of finding in the rough beast that "slouches towards Bethlehem to be born" an image of the mock-renaissance that decadence will bring. His poetry is full of anguish over the world's decadence in poem after poem:

> Though the great song return no more
> There's keen delight in what we have:
> The rattle of pebbles on the shore
> Under the receding wave.
> ("The Nineteenth Century and After")

When Edward VII is crowned he writes,

> I have forgot awhile
> Tara uprooted, and new commonness
> Upon the throne and crying about the streets
> And hanging its paper flowers from post to post.
> ("In the Seven Woods")

But it was not only English decadence he resented; it was Irish decadence too, as in "Romantic Ireland's dead and gone, / It's with O'Leary in the grave," or, more largely, "Many ingenious lovely things are gone." Yet he never loses hope, and a renaissance is almost always in the offing. "Easter 1916," which declares that "A terrible beauty is born," makes the claim that in tragic failure Ireland has achieved heroic rebirth. The great sacrifice is a true Easter, as the poet is the first to recognise.

Yeats identified decadence, much as Wilde did, as all the things that the Victorians celebrated as evidences of health. He spoke derisively of "that decadence we call progress." The Victorian poets had allowed morality and religion to fill their art with impurities, such as the "doctrine of sincerity." Victorian morality was particularly blameworthy. So he says in *A Vision* (1925), "A decadence will descend, by perpetual moral improvement, upon a community which may seem like some woman of New York or Paris who has renounced her rouge pot to lose her figure." He insisted even in his early work that fantasy and caprice would lose their necessary freedom if united either with good or with evil. Wilde sometimes referred distantly to a *higher ethics*, which would completely revise moral standards, and Yeats was prompted to try to redefine good and evil, in terms of an aesthetic point of view. In *A Vision* (1925) he said that, for men of the coming age, good would be that "which a man can contemplate himself as doing always and no other doing at all." This definition underlies poems such as the ones in which Yeats sanctions "the wild old wicked man," or praises Crazy Jane against the Bishop, or pleads for vital personality instead of dead character, for laughter instead of solemnity. For he too, like Wilde, knew the terrible unimportance—or even danger—of being earnest. Artists are in league with lovers because they too are in search of an amplified consciousness. Appropriately, however, when Yeats in "Under Ben Bulben" denounces the present,

> Scorn the sort now growing up
> All out of shape from toe to top,
> Their unremembering hearts and heads
> Base-born products of base beds

as if it were not the case that all beds could be called base—or no beds at all, he asks the Irish *poets* to overcome this decadence. It is they who must engender renaissance of the imagination, to rescue "this foul world in its decline and fall,"

> [. . .] gangling stocks grown great, great stocks run dry,
> Ancestral pearls all pitched into a sty,
> Heroic reverie mocked by clown and knave.
>   ("A Bronze Head")

Like Wilde, Yeats insists on the ulterior motive of art to reshape the world in which we live. This renaissance is always in the making. Sometimes it is present in the deeds of great men, in intense love, in images of poets or in the way the language, often clogged and impeded, suddenly begins to dance.

And here we come to recognize that each Yeats poem is likely to begin in decadence, and to end in renaissance. The decay may be physical, as in "The Tower," or "Sailing to Byzantium," or cultural, as in "Nineteen Hundred and Nineteen." There are of course many variations—sometimes the point is to show that apparent decadence is not true decadence, as in "No Second Troy," and sometimes, as in "The Cold Heaven," the decadence continues into the afterworld, where heaven proves to be hell. But in general the poems present decadence in order to overcome it. The mind contends with some decadent fact or thought or image, then puts it aside in favour of some radiant recovery, a renaissance in little. Yeats does the same thing when he takes up whole civilizations, as if they too at recurrent intervals were artistically rescued from decadence. He expresses this idea most powerfully in "The Gyres":

> Conduct and work grow coarse, and coarse the soul,
> What matter? Those that Rocky Face holds dear,
> Lovers of horses and of women, shall,
> From marble of a broken sepulchre,
> Or dark betwixt the polecat and the owl,
> Or any rich, dark nothing disinter
> The workman, noble and saint, and all things run
> On that unfashionable gyre again.

Lovers of horses and of women—Yeats could have said "artists" directly, but he avoids the term, not wishing to be totally aesthetic. The term "artist" had become much less honorific than it was in Wilde's time, yet the artist's role in conjuring up the best of life out of marble or air is implicit.

In Wilde and Yeats "decadence" becomes the term to turn upon their antagonists. The decadents are those who accept the acquisitive, insensitive, unimaginative world, with all its morality, sincerity and seriousness. This world exists only as a distortion of reality, as Blake would also have said. Wilde could celebrate art more directly in his time than was possible in Yeats's more ironical age, and, while Yeats believed as fully as Wilde did that the mind of man can be rescued by art, he had to be wary in praising a faculty that others were quick to belittle. If Yeats is occasionally circumspect, Joyce is even more so. By his time silence, exile and cunning are required. Yet, though he would not have said so, Joyce was in the same tradition.

He rarely discusses decadence or renaissance in general terms as Wilde and Yeats had. The word "aesthetic" was used by him to describe a philosophical theory, not adjectivally to pat art on the back. He even called Yeats an aesthete in a derogatory way, meaning that Yeats had been too ethereal and so had drifted about. Joyce wanted his renaissance closer to earth. He began by particularizing the waste-land qualities of life in Ireland. He has Mr. Dedalus say at the Christmas dinner in *A Portrait*, "A priestridden godforsaken race." In "The Day of the Rabblement," Joyce's first published work, he called the Irish the "most belated race in Europe." Later Stephen Dedalus in *A Portrait* says that Ireland is "the old sow that eats her farrow." Joyce, as a writer of fiction based on close observation, makes a more detailed attack upon hypocrisy than either Wilde or Yeats—he shows his countrymen pretending to piety and goodness but actually using religion and morality to curb individual lives with cruelty and repressiveness. In *Dubliners* he presented his initial indictment of Ireland in terms of its inertness, repression and corruption. Yet *Dubliners* does not rest in the portrayal of decadence. It establishes by tacit antithesis what it is the country lacks. Even while he portrays the fallen state of his countrymen, Joyce introduces three elements of possible relief. The first is a sympathy, usually latent and unstated, for thwarted lives. The second is the evident pleasure taken by the author in Dublin humour. If Joyce were merely excoriating, the humour would be a continual irrelevance. But it is not irrelevant; it keeps suggesting that even squalor can be funny, as if to enable us to withdraw a little from mere disgust or horror, and yet by prodding the muscles with which we laugh to keep us from detachment. Through humour we tumble to our likeness with others. The third is the reserved, fastidious diction and occasional bursts of lyricism. It is as if Joyce were proclaiming that all is chaos, but doing so in heroic couplets. When even the most mentally impoverished situations are described so deftly, so reservedly, so lyrically, the style itself offers the lost rhythms, the missing emotional possibilities, the absent structure. The age weeps, the rhythm smiles. So, as hopes are dashed, enterprises doomed, love unrequited or warped, sympathy, humour and lyricism keep reminding us that life need not necessarily be so incomplete. Joyce is not being inconsistent then, in the last story of *Dubliners*, "The Dead," where his hero is forced to acknowledge that there can be passion in parochialism and primitivism. The country may be decadent, yet still worth saving.

If the description of decadence is by example rather than generalization, so is the description of renaissance. Yet that Joyce hoped for a renaissance was something he did say explicitly, though in less grandiloquent language, on a few rare occasions. The first was in his semi-autobiographical narrative essay entitled "A Portrait of the Artist," not the book that came later. He ends that essay with a promise of what, thanks to the artist, is to come:

> To those multitudes, not as yet in the wombs of humanity but surely engenderable there, he would give the word: Man and woman, out of you comes the nation that is to come, the lightening of your masses in travail; the competitive order is employed against itself, the aristocracies are supplanted, and amid the general paralysis of an insane society, the confederate will issues in action.

The later novel, *A Portrait of the Artist as a Young Man*, uses a different method from *Dubliners* in that decadence is described not from various points of view, but entirely through the growing consciousness of it in mind of the inchoate artist. The criticism of decadence is much the same but looks different because of this focus. Stephen's future depends upon his becoming an artist, but the future of Ireland depends upon it too. So he asks himself, as he thinks of his decadent countrymen, "How could he hit their conscience or how cast his shadow over the imaginations of their daughters, before their squires begat upon them, that they might breed a race less ignoble than their own."

At the book's end, Stephen announces that he is going forth for the millionth time to "encounter the reality of experience and to forge in the smithy of my soul the uncreated conscience of my race." Joyce has stolen conscience away from the Church and given it to art. He wishes to emphasise that his art will work with reality, not Zolaesque reality, which is distortion in the name of the body, and not mystical distortion, which is the name of the soul—but it is through art that he hopes to bring about his great change. As he wrote in a letter to his wife on 22 August 1912, "I am one of the writers of the generation who are perhaps creating at last a conscience in the soul of this wretched race."

Joyce had read Wilde, regarded him as a hero of literature, a victim of society; he had Buck Mulligan mock Wilde's idea of a new hellenism, but what Mulligan mocks is what Joyce doesn't mock. Even if Joyce would not have used that slogan, *Ulysses* with its Greek title was intended to bring something like a new hellenism about. Because *Ulysses* does so many things—Joyce worried at one point whether he was trying to do too much—this basic impulse has been lost. Yet Joyce, like Stephen in *Stephen Hero*, considered art to be the vital centre of life. When he speaks of a conscience he means something different from the conscience then prevalent—something in tune with Wilde's higher ethics, more hellenic than Christian. It is a conscience which is always in search of more freedom for itself, and hence for both artist and his audience. Readers of *Ulysses* have pondered endlessly whether the principal characters are reborn. They do not need to be. Their consciences have gradually defined themselves as exemplary in action and thought against the powers of the world. In "Circe" they resist final attempts to subdue them. They are the race less ignoble than their fellows for which the artist has forged a conscience. Stephen poses the negative aspect of the new era and the new conscience when he points to his head and quotes Blake against subjugation of his spirit or body, "But in here it is I must kill the priest and the king." Bloom poses the affirmative aspect when he advocates "the opposite of force, hatred, history, all that" as truly life—and when pressed says, "Love, I mean the opposite of hatred." Molly Bloom is needed to complete the picture to raise their fragmentariness to lyricism, and to show by her general approval of

Bloom and Stephen that nature, to which she may be a little closer than they, responds to the values of art—sensitivity, discrimination, sympathy, understanding, and intensity of feeling. Although she is described as fleshy, she is not fleshlier than Hamlet. For her too the mind affects everything. The tenor of her thoughts is to acknowledge grudgingly that her husband, who recognises her wit and musical talent and inner nature, is a better man than Blazes Boylan. "I saw he understood or felt what a woman is," she says. Penelope recognizes Ulysses not by his scar but by his imagination. All three characters achieve a freedom from hypocritical spirituality or empty materiality. In reading about them, the reader takes on the new conscience too. Joyce, like Wilde and Yeats, had a fifth gospel, a vision, a new bible. So reading *Ulysses*, if that book is properly understood, is a means of emancipation. One is freed by it to read about freedom.

Decadence, then, had its uses for Wilde, Yeats and Joyce, as a pivot around which they could organize their work. All in their different ways summon up an opposite to decadence, the promise of an "unfashionable" age for which as artists they constitute themselves heralds. They are not decadents but counterdecadents. Or we could say that they went through decadence to come out on the other side.

GUY WILLOUGHBY

A Poetics for Living: Christ and the Meaning of Sorrow in De Profundis

"My life," Oscar Wilde explained to André Gide shortly after his release from Reading Gaol, "is like a work of art; an artist never starts the same thing twice . . . or if he does, it's that he hasn't succeeded. My life before prison was as successful as possible; now it's something that's over."[1] In his monumental attempt at self-revelation called *De Profundis*, written at Reading in 1897 but only published *in toto* some fifty years after his death,[2] Wilde gives spirited expression to the doctrine here encapsulated. Presenting his own troubled history as a self-conscious creation, he adjures his audience to review his life according to the tenets of art-criticism, whereby all his deeds may be faced, condoned, and integrated into a complex and suggestive artifact.

This unique aesthetic *apologia*—so reminiscent of other Victorian confessions of faith or doubt, and yet so different in tone and substance[3]—depends for its effect on a central rhetorical strategy: the speaker's identification with Jesus Christ, who is presented in a series of evocative reflections as the great historical model and inspiration of the writer's reformulated aestheticism. The identification is suggested at climatic points along the highly discursive path of Wilde's narration, so that the optimistic conclusion, its tone of hope and tentative assurance, reads as confirmation of the writer's new Christ-like integrity and humility. In this chapter I begin by examining the central

From *Art and Christhood: The Aesthetics of Oscar Wilde*, pp. 103–18, 153–55. Copyright © 1993 by Associated University Presses.

dissertation on Christ's nature and ministry in order to claim the wider import of Wilde's Christology—both for ethics and aesthetics. Finally I consider this portrait in relation to Wilde's preceding fictional and dramatic work, in order to demonstrate how vividly and comprehensively Wilde's imaginative writings anticipate the transformed aesthetic views of *De Profundis*.

I

In *The Soul of Man*, Jesus had been characterized as the great individual moralist, who "put forward" the idea of pain "as a mode of self-realisation." Now, the apologist extends this definition; not only is Christ "the supreme individualist . . . of history," but he exemplifies "the artistic life," having afforded his own history the complex integrity elsewhere found only in achieved art. Effectively, he is therefore the supreme artist, for "that which is the very keynote of romantic art was to him the proper basis of actual life" (p. 485). Romantic art, asserts the writer in a characteristic synthesis of Coleridgian poetics via Pater,[4] is all work that is made "from within through some spirit informing it" (p. 482), and Christ's life exemplifies this "keynote." In Jesus "we can discern . . . that close union of personality with perfection which forms the real distinction between classical and romantic art, and makes Christ the true precursor of the romantic movement *in life*" (Italics mine; p. 476). Accordingly, "his place is with the poets" (p. 479), because "the strange figures of poetic drama and ballad are made by the imagination of others, but out of his own imagination entirely did Jesus of Nazareth create himself" (p. 482).

Wilde is at pains to demonstrate how Christ's life embodied the author's Romantic views of art. If "truth in art is the unity of a thing with itself" (p. 473), it was Christ who realized that, through the experience of "Sorrow," any individual can transform his or her existence into a correspondingly unique unity:

> Of such modes of existence there are not a few. . . . Music, in which all subject is absorbed in expression and cannot be separated from it, is a complex example, and a flower or a child a simple example of what I mean: but Sorrow is the ultimate type both in life and Art. (p. 473)

Christ, Wilde confirms, provided humanity with the definitive example of this "mode of existence." To Christ, "Sorrow and Suffering were modes through which he could realise his conception of the Beautiful," and his genius was to make his own life a reflection of this insight: "And feeling . . . that an idea is of no value till it becomes incarnate and is made an image, he makes of himself the image of the Man of Sorrows, and as such has fascinated and dominated Art as no Greek god ever succeeded in doing" (p. 481). This image, that of the universal experience of suffering, enables all its spectators past and present to conceive, as Jesus did, "the divided races as a unity" (p. 477).

Here, then, is an elaborately argued explanation of both Christ's motive, and his achievement, that ignores purely theological or moral assumptions. In one sense, Wilde's characterization of Jesus exemplifies the concern of the Romantic poets to transcend, *via* the imagination, the limitations of nature, and the "perfection" Christ realized certainly echoes the recurring Romantic concern with the essential unity of the individual consciousness. It is important to notice, however, that Wilde's original contribution to Romantic poetics effectively qualifies the vague idealism of Romantics such as Blake or Shelley. Like his fellow secular Christologists Ernest Renan and Matthew Arnold, Wilde conceives of Jesus as a charismatic human being, whose original impact on the world has been imaginatively transformed by later generations.[5]

As an undergraduate under the sway of positivist and empirical enthusiasm, Wilde had observed in "The Rise of Historical Criticism" (1879) that the appearance of great individuals in history was invariably followed by mythopoeic accretions that the critic is obliged to decipher.[6] In *De Profundis* he accordingly interprets Christ's miracles as imaginative responses to the "charm of his personality," and cites several ingenious interpretations (p. 478). Wilde's general method is to withstand the intrusion of the supernatural into his schema, and in this way the idealizing tendency of earlier Romantics is filtered through the empirical concerns of his more immediate intellectual mentors.

Wilde advances beyond Arnold and Renan, however, in his claims for Christ's relation to art. "The very basis of his nature," writes Wilde, "was the same as that of the nature of the artist, an intense and flamelike imagination" (p. 476). The artist's ability to transform disparate elements into a complex symmetry, his "sense of beauty," was in Christ an ability to comprehend the inherent oneness of humanity: "He realised in the entire sphere of human relations," the writer continues, "that imaginative sympathy which in the sphere of Art is the sole secret of creation" (p. 476). Unlike Wilde's earlier model aesthetician in "The Critic as Artist," who prizes "contemplation" and a divorcement from active social engagement (*Intentions*, p. 1043), Jesus sought out those who suffered: "Those of whom I have spoken, who are dumb under oppression and 'whose silence is heard only of God,' he chose as his brothers" (p. 481). Such commitment to the "entire sphere of human relations" distinguishes Christ, and the expanded mode of aestheticism he personifies, from both the artist and the earlier "artist-critic" of *Intentions*.

The shift in the grounds of Wilde's aesthetic is highlighted by his judgment of *Marius the Epicurean*, Walter Pater's most ambitious fictional attempt to deal with the ethical consequences of an aesthetic view of life.[7] According to Wilde, Pater failed to reconcile "the artistic life," the life based on aesthetic principles, "with the life of religion" in its ethical sense, because his hero Marius took only a cautious part in "the spectacle of life," with all its moral complexities, in his grave search for a satisfying philosophy (p. 476). Unaware, therefore, of what Wilde calls the "extraordinary reality" of suffering, Marius's limited aesthetic sense is directed only at appearances, "the comeliness of the vessels," and does not enable him "to notice it is the Sanctuary of Sorrow he is gazing at." Wilde, by comparison, promises to draw "a far more intimate and immediate connection between the true life of Christ and the true life of the artist," for in so doing he will propose that a vital aestheticism does indeed take proper account of the trying demands of social existence. Jesus, in short, provided in his own career an aesthetic resolution of the supposed conflict between art and life—a resolution that Pater himself, in the final tentative pages of *Marius the Epicurean*, could barely hint at.

Wilde clarifies his view of Jesus' awesome imagination with reference to St. John's Gospel. The imagination, he declares, is "the basis of all spiritual and material life," and is therefore "simply a form of love" (p. 484). This is Christ's insight, the insight of all who perceive the universality of human suffering, and it is therefore only by a leap of the imagination, not faith, that the mind can comprehend the beautiful integrity that sorrow affords the world. This argument, and its crucial emphasis on the aesthetic sense—the human impulse to order, and to shape—is earlier put with attractive felicity.

> Love is fed by the imagination, by which we become wiser than we know, better than we feel, nobler than we are: by which, and by which alone, we can understand others in their real as in their ideal relations. (p. 445)

The sense here of the world permeated by the shaping force of the "imagination" reflects Wilde's own imaginative response to St. John's Gospel. The opening passages of the Gospel that the writer singles out for special praise (p. 484) may well have suggested, with their formulation of the Word given body, the writer's conception of Jesus as artist.

> [Christ] sees all the lovely influences of life as modes of light: the imagination itself is the world-light, tophostoneosmon: the world is made by it, and yet the world cannot understand it; that is because the imagination is simply a manifestation of Love, and it

is Love, and the capacity for it, that distinguishes one human being from another. (p. 486)

Johannine theology is translated, in effect, into a new aesthetic, and thoroughly humanist, creed: Jesus embodies the synthetic power of the imagination, and invites others to explore their potential, for "it is Love, and the capacity for it, that distinguishes one human being from another."

Christ's profound effect on the imagination of succeeding generations is based, therefore, not on his standing as a moral exemplar per se, but because of his daunting achievement of self-perfection through absolute individualism. Like great art, he "creates that mood by which alone he can be understood" (p. 483), rather than adumbrating an inflexible moral doctrine. For Wilde, he simply wants to awaken his fellows to their own potential; his enduring achievement is to hold out to those who encounter him the idea that human consciousness can transform every possible kind of experience. "It is to me a joy to remember," Wilde observes, in reflecting on Christ's impact on others, "that if he is 'of imagination all compact,' the world itself is of the same substance" (p. 483).

Wilde had made approving reference to Christ's imaginative moral judgments in *The Soul of Man*. Now he goes further, and credits Jesus with a bold and novel insight into the validity of the traditional idea of "sin":

> The world had always loved the Saint as being the nearest possible approach to the perfection of God. Christ . . . seems to have always loved the sinner as being the nearest possible approach to the perfection of man . . . in a manner not yet understood of the world he regarded sin and suffering as being in themselves beautiful, holy things, and modes of perfection. It *sounds* a very dangerous idea. It is so. All great ideas *are* dangerous. That it was Christ's creed admits of no doubt. That it is the true creed, I don't doubt myself. (Wilde's italics, p. 486)

Sin, once described by Gilbert in "The Critic as Artist" as "the colour-element in modern life," the means by which one asserts one's defiance of a post-Darwinian and determinist society (*Intentions*, p. 1023), becomes, in recollection, a vital phase in self-discovery. This is why the sinners Christ forgave "are saved simply for beautiful moments in their lives" (p. 486); the moment of repentance is also the moment of acceptance, the means by which one comes closer to realizing the full range and extent of one's intellectual and emotional resources. "Repentance" is a vital component of the experience of sin, if that experience is to be properly assessed, valued, and then integrated into the completed artwork of one's history:

> Of course the sinner must repent. But why? Simply because
> otherwise he would be unable to realise what he had done. The
> moment of repentance is the moment of initiation. More than that.
> It is the means by which one alters one's past. . . . Christ, had he
> been asked, would have said—I feel quite certain about it—that the
> moment the prodigal son fell on his knees and wept he really made
> his having wasted his substance with harlots, and then kept swine
> and hungered for the husks they ate, beautiful and holy things in
> his life. (p. 487)

In formulating this special virtue of sin, Wilde draws on a number of Gnostic sources on the fringes of orthodox Christian theology, and reflects, too, the recurring obsession of such later Romantics as Baudelaire and Verlaine, who sought to discover in the consciousness of degradation the elements of a new and purified selfhood.[8]

For Wilde, of course, the commitment to an *aesthetic* apprehension of something that resembles Christian repentance is foremost. Wilde cites Christ's moral judgments in the Gospels as persuasive arguments for this view: Mary Magdalene, in breaking the vase of perfume over Christ's feet, is expressing the "beautiful moment" of her realization of sin (p. 486). In these sonorous and evocative passages, Wilde offers his most extended explanation of his private view in the letter to Mrs. Lathbury that the saint and the hedonist "meet—touch in many points"; the sinner, indeed, becomes the saint, and these extreme human tendencies are merged in a new model of consciousness that corresponds in impact to the work of art.

Perhaps the most fascinating and richly suggestive aspect of the Christ of *De Profundis* is his role as reconciler of Hellenism and Hebraicism. As we have seen, the tension Matthew Arnold had espied between these currents in European thought runs throughout Wilde's work, especially as he tended to trace his aesthetic concerns, as did Pater, back to the Greeks. At the conclusion of *The Soul of Man* Wilde refers to the individualism of the future as "the New Hellenism" from which Jesus, the avatar of Hebraic responsibilities and "the worship of pain," is summarily banished. But throughout the later meditation on Christ, Wilde establishes a series of telling contrasts and comparisons between Jesus' life and values, and those of the Greeks, which confirms Christ's achievement of a novel synthesis. The inescapable conclusion is that the man who was "the precursor of the romantic movement in life" fused the ethical concerns of the Jews with the aesthetic impulse of the Greeks, and created in himself a potent symbol of a future ideal culture. In so doing he revealed the limitations of the old Hellenic culture that he echoes and yet replaces.

Early on in his presentation of Jesus, Wilde remarks that his life "has fascinated and dominated art as no Greek god ever did" because, in spite of their comely appearances, "the white and red of their fair fleet limbs," the Hellenic deities actually epitomized such vices as cruelty, pride, and lust (p. 481). While the Greek genius could produce no gods that could inspire real admiration and love, "Out of the carpenter's shop at Nazareth had come a personality infinitely greater than any made by myth and legend" (p. 481). Significantly, the only "deep suggestive figures of Greek mythology" were the fertility deities Demeter and Dionysus, both of whom were traditionally associated with rebirth and regeneration, as well as the propagation and development of human culture.

Yet, notable as these figures were for the progress of humanity, for "religion" and for "art," they were outmoded by the human Jesus, who conflates the religious and artistic urges of his species in his own life and ministry. Wilde metaphorically renders this supersession by pointing out how the symbols of natural growth and human industry traditionally connected with Demeter and Dionysus were given a distinctive impress by Christ: He was "destined to reveal to the world the mystical meaning of wine and the real beauty of the lilies of the field as none, either on Cithaeron or at Enna, had ever done it" (p. 481).

This transformation of imagery represents in symbolic terms the superior vision of Christ over that of the most "suggestive" Hellenic deities. Wine, the symbol of Dionysus, and of the art of viticulture he taught to men and women, is transformed by Wilde's Jesus into a vital image of his own sacrifice for humanity; the flowers in the meadows of Enna from which Pluto, in seizing Demeter's daughter Persephone, initiated the mythic story of seasonal rebirth associated with Demeter, become as "the lilies of the field" images of the beautiful integrity Christ espouses to his fellows. Christ, in effect, being the great archetypal romantic artist-in-life, imbues the natural world with a far profounder symbolism than the Greeks, for all their devotion to self-development, could attain.

Having compared Christ's rich symbolic usage of nature with that of the Greek idyllic poets (p. 481), Wilde asserts that the Galilean's unique Hebraic valuation of "sin" powerfully transcended the Hellenic approach to conduct, with its marked fatalism. Wilde's interpretation of Christ's creed stresses that the Hebraic genius for right action could be fused with the Hellenic emphasis on beauty:

> The moment of repentance is the moment of initiation. More than that. It is the means by which one alters one's past. The Greeks thought that impossible. They often say in their gnomic aphorisms

"Even the gods cannot alter the past." Christ showed that the
commonest sinner could do it. That it was the one thing he could
do. (p. 487)

It is clear from the juxtaposition of Greek and Christian ethical perspectives—Wilde is quoting loosely from Aristotle and Pindar[9]—that Christ's
conception of self-realization was a far more dynamic one, that it took a
much broader account of the range of experiences and viewpoints available
to the individual, and that a Greek ideal like "self-perfection" only really
becomes possible when the Hebraic insistence on morality and repentance
are incorporated. Once again Christ is the great artist whose breadth of
imagination enables him to weave this finer model of self-perfection from
the rival strands of European thought.

Wilde also points out, following Renan,[10] that Christ's advent fulfilled
certain yearnings of the Classical world, as well as of the Hebraic. For while
Jesus took his suggestion for self-creation as "the Man of Sorrows" from the
Song of Isaiah, and thus seemed to fulfill Jewish prophecy, his appearance
was also prefigured in Roman literature (pp. 481–82). While he insists that
Jesus was not necessarily fulfilling some divine plan, but merely responding
in his own way to an idea in his people's prophetic literature—"For every
expectation that he fulfilled, there was another he destroyed "—Wilde's cross-
reference to Virgil's predictions in his fourth Eclogue[11] reinforces the reader's
sense of Christ's synthetic achievement.

It is fitting, therefore, that Wilde indicates that his view of Jesus is
largely drawn from the Gospel of St. John, "or whatever early Gnostic took
his name and mantle" (p. 484), for—as the qualification I have quoted indicates—that gospel has been regarded, since D. W. Strauss's epoch-making
Leben Jesu (1835), as most permeated with Greek thought.[12] By relating
Christ's romantic imagination: to the "world-light" that makes and dwells in
the world (St. *John*, 1:1–12), Wilde emphasizes the neo-Platonic contribution
to our traditional understanding of Jesus, and lends credence to his own view
that Christ's meaning incorporates both Hellenic and Hebraic elements.

Further, Wilde cites the particular pleasure of reading the Gospels in
the Greek language; not only does it realert us to "the *naïveté*, the freshness,
the simple romantic charm" of these testaments (p. 483), but "it is extremely
probable that we have the actual terms, the *ipsissima verba*, used by Christ" (p.
483). Drawing on contemporary theories that Greek was the *lingua franca* of
the entire ancient world,[13] Wilde advances a pleasant fancy that, metaphorically, suggests the reconciliation Jesus achieves. "It is a delight to me to think,"
he continues, "that as far as his conversation was concerned, Charmides might
have listened to him, and Socrates reasoned with him, and Plato understood

him" (p. 483). By way of corroborating his theory, Wilde then quotes appreciatively from his Greek Testament those utterances of Christ that echo the aphoristic style and pastoral setting of much Greek literature. His gloss of St. John's version of Christ's death serves two purposes. It affirms Wilde's belief in Christ's humanity, by omitting the possibility of resurrection, and it confirms that Jesus consciously achieved that "self-perfection" the Greeks had sought: "his last word when he cried out 'My life has been completed, has reached its fulfilment, has been perfected,' was exactly as St. John tells us it was: tetelestai: no more" (p. 483–84).

The most remarkable aspect of Christ's great work of synthesis is in Wilde's discourse on his life as "the most wonderful of poems" (p. 477). The tragic elements in his history outclass any achievement in literature, transcending, in particular, all the Aristotelian categories of Greek drama (p. 478). Yet Christ's life is not merely the greatest tragedy in the European tradition; its total meaning is more richly affirmative, and responds to an ancient ancestral memory.

> Yet the whole life of Christ—so entirely may Sorrow and Beauty be made one in their meaning and manifestation—is really an idyll, though it ends with the veil of the temple being rent, and the darkness coming over the face of the earth, and the stone rolled away from the sepulchre. One always thinks of him as a young bridegroom with his companions, as indeed he somewhere describes himself, or as a shepherd straying through a valley with his sheep in search of green meadow or cool stream, or as a singer trying to build out of music the walls of the city of God, or as a lover for whose love the whole world was too small. (p. 478)

Here Wilde calls into play the entire pastoral tradition in Greek poetry, including the transformation of sadness at death into joyous acceptance that elegiac poetry records. Wilde refers to the various rural personae Jesus chooses for himself in the Gospel—the "young bridegroom," "the shepherd," "the singer," "the lover"—all of which correspond to the conventional aspects of the shepherd-poet who is both the creator of the Greek idyll and the principal performer in it, just as Christ is in relation to his own life.[14] Wilde's image of Christ the pastoral singer whose life was his song therefore represents a powerful and suggestive attempt to close, with reference to a venerable literary convention, the Hellenic-Hebraic divide that concerned Arnold and Pater.

In terms of the elegiac form of the idyll, Wilde's characterization of Christ is especially apposite. The analogies between Adonis, the slain fertility god who is the original subject of the elegy, and Jesus are obvious, and Wilde does not have to spell out this rich vein of continuity between Classical and Christian literature.

But there is a further powerful way in which Wilde's reference to idyllic conventions extends his view of Christ, for the elegy enshrines a paradox. It represents a powerful example of human artistry, becoming, indeed, an image of our creative ability to transcend experience.[15] Accordingly, we may see Christ's life as a great elegy, evidence that—in Wilde's words—"Sorrow and Beauty [may] be made one in their meaning and manifestation"; that life is the ultimate vindication of the aesthetic view, whereby the most shattering emotions and episodes in one's experience may be integrated into a total design where global form dictates final content, where "manifestation" becomes "meaning." Likewise, Christ's history affirms that, like all the singer-performers of the pastoral tradition, one must consciously create this design oneself. So it is that Jesus "makes of himself the image of the Man of Sorrows, and as such has fascinated and dominated Art as no Greek god ever succeeded in doing" (p. 481).

In his awesome comprehension of the fullness of human experience, and of the great effort of consciousness needed to integrate it, Christ, for Wilde, succeeds in recharging Hellenism with his own vision.

> He is charming when he says, "take no thought for the morrow. Is not the *soul* more than meat? It not the *body* more than raiment?" A Greek might have said the latter phrase. It is full of Greek feeling. But only Christ could have said both, and so summed up life perfectly for us. [Wilde's italics] (p. 485)

Wilde's Christ, in the final estimation, achieves a series of reconciliations, each of which overlaps with and complements the others. Ethics dissolves into aesthetics; piety is absorbed into practice; Hebraicism and Hellenism combine; the gap closes between life and art. However doubtful the author's own claims to creative discipleship may be at the end of *De Profundis*, the power, insight, and surprise of his final portrait of the man Jesus reads as a complex coda to a body of work that enshrines a determination to save the Nazarean for a secular world, and to recharge that world with the integrity of art.

> Indeed, that is the charm of Christ, when all is said. He is just like a work of art himself. He does not really teach one anything, but by being brought into his presence one becomes something. And everybody is predestined to his presence. Once at least in his life each man walks with Christ to Emmaus. (p. 487)

II

In the context of *De Profundis*, the function of the exposition on Jesus is to suggest that the author is nearing, through the force of his experiences, a Christlike state of self-knowledge. Like Jesus, the writer has been faced with "the hard Hedonists . . . those who waste their freedom in becoming slaves to things" (p. 480), as vividly personified in the person of Lord Alfred Douglas; like Jesus also, he has taken over "in pity and kindness" his friend's responsibilities (p. 425), and in the process has lost everything himself—family, reputation, livelihood, even personal liberty. Yet his aim, he repeats to his correspondent throughout, is to resist any feelings of bitterness or resentment, especially toward the man whose selfishness, he claims, has caused this downfall. Douglas's culpability, too, must also be imaginatively assumed, even in these circumstances: "I cannot allow you to go through life bearing in your heart the burden of having ruined a man like me . . . I must take the burden from you and put it onto my shoulders" (p. 465). Like Christ, in effect, he must refrain from censuring his adversary, but rather try to awaken the dormant imagination that prevents Douglas from understanding his own conduct. His constant iteration, therefore, is that "the supreme vice is shallowness. Whatever is realised is right."

Whatever our assessment of this identification with Christ—and it can certainly be argued that Wilde mars his rhetorical purpose by lapses into self-pity and recrimination at various points in his discourse—it is important to understand the resolution toward which the writer is moving. Wilde is suggesting that, by accepting all his punishing experience with full humility, he will attain the complex perfection that only Christ, and his most imaginative and selfless followers, have ever achieved. Like the prodigal son, who by facing the viciousness of his deeds transformed them into "beautiful and holy incidents in his life" (p. 487), the writer hopes to discover a profound new affinity with the entire human and natural world (pp. 509–10). He emphasizes throughout, moreover, the major lesson that Christ in *De Profundis* embodies: only personal experience and discovery of these realities is of value.

> Nor am I making any demands on Life. In all that I have said I am simply concerned with my own mental attitude towards life as a whole: and I feel that not to be ashamed of having been punished is one of the first points I must attain to, for the sake of my own perfection, and because I am so imperfect. (p. 471)

Whether or not the writer will succeed in bringing, as a consequence, "a still deeper note, one of greater unity of passion, and directness of impulse" into his art (p. 489), he is ready now to transfer his insights to conduct and to become, like Jesus, an artist in life. Having had all externals taken away from him, he may regain in their place an inner completion hitherto unknown to him:

> But so my portion has been meted out to me; and during the last two months I have, after terrible struggles and difficulties, been able to comprehend some of the lessons hidden in the heart of pain. Clergymen, and people who use phrases without wisdom, sometimes talk of suffering as a mystery. It is really a revelation. One discerns things that one never discerned before. One approaches the whole of history from a different standpoint. What one had felt dimly through instinct, about Art, is intellectually and emotionally realised with perfect clearness of vision and absolute intensity of apprehension. (p. 473)

What he "had felt dimly" about Art was exactly that wholeness which sorrow affords life: the "revelation" of his traumatic experience is his new awareness that, when the aesthetic sense is operative in actual conduct, it is sorrow that is seen to accord life a wonderful completion, to suggest, in the words quoted toward the beginning of his dissertation on Christ, "that mode of existence in which soul and body are one and indivisible: in which the outward is expressive of the inward: in which Form reveals" (p. 473).

Wilde's delineation of Christ, and the elaborate act of identification that accompanies it, throws his preceding fictive evocations of the Galilean into vivid relief. When he writes, at a point in his dissertation on Jesus, that there are two subjects he would like to write about in the future—"one is 'Christ, as the precursor of the Romantic movement in life': the other is 'the Artistic life considered in its relation to Conduct'" (p. 484)—the irony is twofold. Not only do the subjects of Christ and the "Artistic life" combine in *De Profundis* itself, but the stories, dramas, and parables examined in this study presage these more explicit formulations. Under different specifics of plot, genre, and setting, each fable confirms that individual realization depends, ultimately, on a full and unabashed knowledge of the intrinsic pain and reversal of human existence; that true beauty or completeness of self begins in the denial of the superficial attractions that the world may offer in place of human involvement; and that Christ is the archetype for this acknowledgment and the mode of life that flows from it.

In the prose fiction, the poetic dramas, and the *Poems in Prose*, various false modes of hedonism are dramatized, but those who are committed to such gratifications fail to achieve that "perfection through joy" that the confident essayist of *The Soul of Man* espouses. *Dorian Gray* presents the most ambitious yet complete failure of a narrow aestheticism. The titular hero's despair and distraction resembles that of the Tetrarch Herod and the Man in "The House of Judgement," lost in a self-created limbo of spent will and desire: "Never, and in no place," says the condemned Man, "Have I been able to imagine [Heaven]." The more fortunate hedonists advance, like Wilde himself in *De Profundis*, to a Christlike realization of wider suffering, and imaginatively transform this apprehension into a personal knowledge. The heroes of *The Happy Prince* and *Pomegranates* exemplify this imaginative assumption, and the greater selfhood it engenders; Salome unconsciously approaches it, when in her anguish she cries out that "Love is greater than death. Only love should one consider." Myrrhina is the fully achieved *sainte courtisane*, who consciously changes her entire mode of life once the search for pleasure has been revealed as a "painted mask" over the mysteries of love and death.

Of course, the Happy Prince and the Little Swallow are innocent exemplars of the change from selfish insularity to a Christlike intercourse and exchange with the world; both statue and bird are to be partly rewarded by eternal residence in a more wonderful version of the walled garden the Happy Prince inhabited in life, a rather literal sounding "City of Gold" in which they will eternally praise God. Similarly, the Young King apparently becomes a resident of such a city, too, as he returns to his palace with "the face of an angel" and a glittering *ensemble* of seeming jewels and gold leaf. While the enigmatic resolutions of "The Fisherman and His Soul" and "The Star Child" imply less straightforward relations between will and achievement, such obvious rewards become less tangible in the still more stylized versions of this paradigm written after *The Soul of Man*. "Heaven," for the Man in "The House of Judgement," has shrunk to the operations of a single mind—as indeed, Hell has also. In "The Teacher of Wisdom," the enigmatic wholeness-through-loss that Christ personifies cannot be represented in material terms, and the title character's analogies with a "pearl of great price" and a "vesture without seam" are ironic reductions that he has to abandon in order to understand his master Jesus. Likewise, the Teacher of Wisdom cannot ascend, in the manner of the Happy Prince, to what he calls "the uttermost courts of God," but will embrace the more exacting life of the world.

Further, the surround in which these journeys to self-discovery take place also changes, from the idyllic setting of "The Selfish Giant" or "The Nightingale and the Rose" to the corrupt and fractured worlds of Herod's court and of Alexandrian Egypt, in which the lures of hedonism have become altogether more sinister and beguiling. Dorian Gray's contemporary world contains both sides of the Wildean milieu: the Edenic reaches of Basil Hallward's Mayfair garden and the sordid underworld of the East End. The novel pivots between fairy tale and decadent drama, between aesthetic dream and decadent nightmare. In this context, the Happy Prince at play in the sunlit confines of *Sans Souci* may stand as an innocent aesthete of the 1880s to Salome's decadent of the nineties, who has to struggle for self-expression in an altogether more complex setting. The *Poems in Prose* moreover represent the hazards and pervasive malaise such a hedonistic milieu fosters. The action of "The Doer of Good" confirms what is implied in "The Happy Prince" and "The Young King": a would-be Christlike disciple will be hard-pressed to prevail in a world of such manifest temptations, while "The Master," indeed, inscribes a warning that self-regard may even take the guise of Christian discipleship.

Such complexities, however, only confirm the vital currency of Christ's message for these jaded habitués—even for those who, like the characters in "The Doer of Good," have lapsed into the habits of a sybaritic world. Through the very intensity of their lifestyles, these later figures may be closer to the profundity of sorrow than their self-important ascetic counterparts, who are too often—like the Baptist, the Thebaid dweller, and the Teacher of Wisdom—cleft in a false image of their own righteousness. The plights of Myrrhina, Salome, and the Robber in "The Teacher of Wisdom" confirm Wilde's view in *De Profundis*, that Christ understands how the intensity of sin may be imaginatively transformed into the elements of a new self-realization; that "Riches and Pleasure seemed to him to be really greater tragedies than Poverty and Sorrow" (p. 480).

In *The Soul of Man* Wilde had carelessly dismissed the Christian ideals of "abandon[ing]" or "resist[ing]" society, but in *De Profundis* the writer resolutely rephrases the Christian ideal to the world, and thereby presages a far more dynamic transformation of society and the individual than the glib prescriptions of "Socialism" and "Science" in the earlier essay really allow. In focusing at last on the inner change that must shape all wider conduct, the writer of *De Profundis* is in accord with the "secret" of Arnold's Jesus—except that, of course, for Wilde the imaginative feat involved is an initiation into a more complex mode of aesthetic apprehension rather than a moral enactment per se. The societal transformation anticipated in "The Young King" and "The Star-Child" becomes, in *De Profundis*, the brief and province of all those who realize with Jesus the indivisible nature of humanity, "the divided races as a unity." As we shall see in the final chapter, *The Ballad of Reading Gaol* represents the author's most overt attempt to transpose that vision into resolutely social terms—an attempt that involves, most strikingly, a novel poetics of direct utterance.

Ultimately, Christ's function in the fairy tales, *Salome, Courtisane,* and "The Teacher of Wisdom" is to personify the shaping power of the imagination, "by which, and through which," says the writer of *De Profundis*, "we can understand others in their real, as in their ideal relations" (p. 445). This fundamentally aesthetic practice is the "secret" of Jesus, the real sense in which, as Wilde asserted in *The Soul of Man*, the Galilean's essential message to humanity was "Be thyself." To be oneself, the Happy Prince and the Young Hermit discover, is to be all others simultaneously; for "while Christ did not say to us, 'Live for others,' he pointed out that there was no difference at all between the lives of others and one's own life." Consequently, "since his coming the history of each separate individual is, or can be made, the history of the world" (p. 480).

Wilde himself insists in *De Profundis* on the place of these themes in his preceding work. His new understanding of the integrality of life, suffering, and the world lends his writings a unity, and—as he had insouciantly predicted in "The Decay of Lying"—he finds his life has imitated his art. "Of course all this is foreshadowed and prefigured in my art," he writes.

> Some of it is in "The Happy Prince": some of it in "The Young King" . . . a great deal of it is hidden away in the note of Doom that like a purple thread runs through the gold cloth of *Dorian Gray:* in "The Critic as Artist" it is set forth in many colours: in *The Soul of Man* it is written down simply and in letters too easy to read: it is one of the refrains whose recurring *motifs* make *Salome* so like a piece of music and bind it together as a ballad. (p. 475)

It now remains to the creator of these self-revelatory fables to enact them in the world, and at the end of *De Profundis* the author serves notice that he, too, will translate Christ's vision of the indivisible and suffering world into conduct. Like Christ he will become the supreme artist whose daily existence will have the penetrating coherence and symmetry that, like the "marvellous, many-petalled rose" of art in Vivian's analogy, will offer a suggestion of completeness to all imaginative spectators. In the last analysis the author-as-subject offers himself as the Christlike hero of his own narrative, and both exemplifies and supersedes all others. His traumatic relationship with Alfred Douglas has become, like Charles Kingsley's accusations of Dr. Newman, the occasion for a new definition of the Christlike self.[16] Like the eloquent defender of the Catholic faith, the author of this aesthetic *apologia* writes, in his concluding paragraph, to a wider audience beyond his correspondent:[17]

> What lies before me is my past. I have got to make myself look on that with different eyes, to make the world look on it with different eyes, to make God look on it with different eyes. This I cannot do by ignoring it, or slighting it, or praising it, or denying it. It is only

to be done by fully accepting it as an inevitable part of the evolution of my life and character: by bowing my head to everything that I have suffered. How far away I am from the true temper of soul, this letter in its changing, uncertain moods, its scorn and bitterness, its aspirations and its failure to realise those aspirations, shows you quite clearly. But do not forget in what a terrible school I am sitting at my task. And incomplete, imperfect, as I am, yet from me you may have still much to gain. You came to me to learn the Pleasure of Life and the Pleasure of Art. Perhaps I am chosen to teach you something much more wonderful, the meaning of Sorrow, and its Beauty.

Your affectionate friend
OSCAR WILDE

Notes

1. As recorded by Gide in his memoir *Oscar Wilde* (trans. Bernard Frechtman; London: William Kimber, 1951), p. 33.

2. This long letter, ostensibly written to the author's friend Lord Alfred Douglas, was composed under exacting conditions at Reading between January and March 1897. Wilde handed it to his future literary executor, Robert Ross, upon his release in May, with a covering letter indicating his desire that it be published—at least in expurgated form—at some future date. Ross accordingly published a severely edited version after the author's death (Methuen, 1905, 1908), and presented the original to the British Museum on the condition no one be allowed to see it for fifty years (1909). The complete letter consequently first appeared in *The Letters of Oscar Wilde*. All page references in this chapter are to this edition.

3. The autobiography had become a major literary paradigm by the last quarter of the century, as individual writers strove to create a composite image of themselves against a backdrop of religious and philosophical turbulence. Noteworthy examples Wilde would have known include Thomas Carlyle's *Sartor Resartus* (1834), J. S. Mill's *Autobiography* (1873), John Ruskin's *Praeterita* (1889), and Walter Pater's *A Child in the House* (1895). Jan B. Gordon has traced the analogies between *De Profundis* and J. H. Newman's *Apologia Pro Vita Sua* (1864), a spiritual autobiography of which Wilde was especially fond ("Wilde and Newman: The Confessional Mode," *Renascence*, XXII, 4, 1970).

4. Pater translated Coleridge's organicism into purely aesthetic terms in his essay on "Style," in *Appreciations* (London: Macmillan, 1889). Wilde commented favorably on this essay in his review of *Appreciations*. See "Mr. Pater's Last Volume," in *The Speaker*, 1, 6, (8 February 1890); repr. in *Reviews*, pp. 538–45.

5. Wilde's meditation on Christ in *De Profundis* contains passing tributes to Renan and Arnold: the Breton's *Vie de Jesus* is referred to as "that gracious Fifth Gospel, the Gospel according to St. Thomas one might call it" (p. 479)—an apposite compliment, as Renan himself praised the Galilean countryside through which he had traveled in 1862 as being "the Fifth Gospel" because of the light it shed on the circumstances of Christ's ministry (*La Vie*, p. 28). "The true temper" of the artist, furthermore, is compared by Wilde to "what Matthew Arnold called the secret of Jesus" (p. 477). This evokes directly Arnold's depiction of Christ in *Literature and*

Dogma: "But there remains the question what righteousness really is. The method and secret and sweet reasonableness of Jesus" (chapter XII).

6. See "The Rise of Historical Criticism," in *Complete Works*, especially pp. 1130–31. This essay was originally written for the Chancellor's Essay prize at Oxford (1879) and was not published in the author's lifetime. A number of commentators have drawn attention to Wilde's mature and informed historical sense in this paean to the "Hellenic" spirit of rational enquiry. E. San Juan believes that it "anticipates modern archetypal criticism and the discipline of cultural anthropology in its respect and appreciation for other civilizations" ("Aesthetics and Literary Criticism," in *The Art of Oscar Wilde*, p. 97).

7. Pater's gesture in his novel toward an acknowledgment of moral obligation is perceptively analyzed by U. Knopfelmacher, in *Religious Humanism and the Victorian Novel* (Princeton, N.J.: Princeton University Press, 1963).

8. Both French poets are appreciatively mentioned in *De Profundis*: Baudelaire is representative of the modern spirit (p. 480), and Verlaine is called "the first Christian poet since Dante," a man who perfected his life in spite of lengthy incarceration (p. 480). Another probable contemporary model for Wilde is Dostoyevsky, who likewise sought to garner from censure and imprisonment a religious ethic of transfiguration. George Woodcock points out that Wilde, as a reviewer, had: applauded the all-embracing "pity" of the Russian novelist, "for those who do evil as well as for those who suffer," as the distinguishing characteristic of his knowledge of "life in its most real forms" ("A Batch of Novels," *Pall Mall Gazette*, 2 May 1887; repr. in *Reviews*, p. 159). See Woodcock, "Paganism and Christianity," p. 77.

9. Hart-Davis compares Wilde's gloss to Aristotle, *Ethics*, VI, 2 and Pindar, *Olympia*, II, 17. See *Letters*, p. 487, fn. 1.

10. *La Vie*, p. 56.

11. Hart-Davis, *Letters*, p. 482, fn. 1.

12. Strauss observes that John substitutes the Hellenic notion of Divine Sonship for the Jewish Messianic conception, and in his emphasis on Christ's presence in the hearts of his followers, rather than on his Second Coming, the Alexandrian *Logos* doctrine and neo-Platonic ideas about preexistence are evident. See Albert Schweitzer's discussion of this question in *The Quest of the Historical Jesus*, trans. W. Montgomery (London: Adam and Charles Black, 1911), pp. 86–88.

13. Wilde demonstrates his acquaintance with contemporary German theology in this remark. See Schweitzer, "Questions Concerning the Aramaic Language," in *The Quest of the Historical Jesus*, pp. 269–79.

14. The grafting of Jesus onto the shepherd-singer of the idyllic convention in Medieval and Renaissance poetry is considered by Peter V. Marinelli, *Pastoral* (London: Methuen, 1971), and Helen Cooper, *Pastoral: Medieval into Renaissance* (Ipswich: D. S. Brewer, 1977).

15. My remarks on the Pastoral are informed by H. E. Toliver's comprehensive study of this subject (*Pastoral Forms and Attitudes*, Los Angeles. University of California Press, 1971). Wilde's acquaintance with this tradition, which derived from his undergraduate studies in *litterae humaniores* at Oxford, is demonstrated in the themes and format of his early poetry (*Poems*, 1881). See, in this connection, "The Last Endymion," in Rodney Shewan's *Oscar Wilde: Art and Egoism* (Macmillan, 1977).

16. Cf. Jan B. Gordon: "The effectiveness of both Newman's *Apologia* and *De Profundis* depends on the way in which each man gives an account of how his mind

'moved' to conviction, so that the reader can be persuaded of its honesty" ("Wilde and Newman: The Confessional Mode," p. 185). For the youthful Wilde's near-conversion to Rome, see note 5 to the Appendix.

17. In a covering letter to Robert Ross, Wilde makes it clear that *De Profundis* is intended, ultimately, for posterity: "Some day the truth will have to be known: not necessarily in my lifetime or in Douglas's: but I am not prepared to sit in the grotesque pillory they put me into for all time" (Letter to Ross from H. M. Prison, Reading, 1 April 1897, *Letters*, p. 512). As well as sending a copy of the letter to Douglas, Wilde instructs Ross to extract certain passages (including substantially the dissertation on Christ and the nature of sorrow) for private distribution to friends (*Letters*, pp. 513–14). From these passages Ross prepared the expurgated *De Profundis* that was published posthumously (London: Methuen, 1905).

RONALD KNOWLES

Bunburying with Bakhtin: A Carnivalesque Reading of The Importance of Being Earnest

'One has a right to Bunbury anywhere one chooses. Every serious Bunburyist knows that.'[1]

Algernon's above claim in *The Importance of Being Earnest* is also good for the critic. 'Visiting' the fictitious valetudinarian, Mr Bunbury, Algy roams the counties of England evading the constraints of London society. Analogously, the critic of today, surveying the theoretical landmarks of the last twenty-five years, is free to Bunbury at will, no longer constrained by the well-trodden footpaths of yesteryear. Here it is proposed, as indicated by the title, to 'Bunbury' with Mikhail Bakhtin and his theories of carnival which are elaborated in his now famous work *Rabelais and His World*[2]. Yet of all influential theorists Bakhtin would appear to be the least relevant here since his extensive study is concerned primarily with the culture of the Middle Ages and the Renaissance, and would seem to have little to do with the most famous comedy of the 1890s. Bakhtin is specifically concerned with pre-capitalist folk culture while Wilde goes out of his way to identify the post-rentier form of late nineteenth-century high capitalism in the upper-class society of his play. However, Bakhtin's investigation into earlier culture is sometimes defined in contrast to the modern world and he also occasionally anticipates the relegated and attenuated transformations of carnival literature in the eighteenth and nineteenth centuries. Conversely,

From *Essays in Poetics* 20 (Autumn 1995): 170–81. Copyright © 1995 by Ronald Knowles.

Wilde's play may be defined in comparison and contrast with the Russian, particularly in terms of the wit of moral and social inversion, that *mundus inversus* of carnival, not to mention the play as a whole as a form of licensed carnival in the London of the 1890s. All of which begs the fascinating critical question—what happens when Bakhtin's ideas and Wilde's play are brought together?

In his introductory chapter Bakhtin outlines the basis of his approach to what he sees as Rabelais' 'world'. There are two principal concepts, that of carnival and the grotesque, which are linked by the literal and metaphorical human body. Bakhtin conceives an oppositional folk culture the expression of which is humour:

> All these forms of protocol and ritual based on laughter and consecrated by tradition existed in all the countries of medieval Europe; they were sharply distinct from the serious, official, ecclesiastical, feudal and political cult forms and ceremonials. They offered a completely different, non-official, extra-ecclesiastical and extra-political aspect of the world, of man, and of human relations; they built a second world in which all medieval people participated more or less, in which they lived during a given time of the year. (pp. 5–6)

Presumably the humanist primitivism of this springs from a retroactive idealised Marxism. However, by means of carnival, populist subversion is licensed by inversion, 'the world turned upside down' as it was in the ancient Roman Saturnalia when there were . . . No more masters, no more servants, no more slaves, no more work, no more private property . . . Everybody put on the clothes of others as he pleased and ate and drunk his bellyful.'[3] Carnival was public, taking place in the town square, when inversions took the form

> of a continual shifting from top to bottom, from front to rear, of numerous parodies and travesties, humiliations, profanations, comic crownings and uncrownings. (p. 11)

The concept of the body retains its resonant organic naturalism yet is conceived collectively. Pre-dating the atomized bourgeois ego of capitalist society, here the collective body of society is writ large on the giant Gargantua, constituting a 'grotesque realism' in Bakhtin's phrase, as against the latter day neoclassical mimesis of nineteenth-century 'realism' (see pp 24–5, 52–3). In a sense Bakhtin's idea is like a parodic inversion of Jung's collective unconscious. In the culture of carnival everyone actively participates in a collective body indulging the orifices in the crucial activities of eating and drinking, copulation and defecation. These, in turn, are part of a unified cycle of birth, life and death. In the materialism of this *weltanschauung* death does not separate the soul from the body, but fertilizes the earth in what is a rebirth (p. 327). In addition to these brief glimpses of Bakhtin's concepts two more ideas need to be brought in here, namely the significance of eating and speech.

Eating in the public collective form of feasting or banqueting is an essential part of carnival, so much so that Bakhtin devotes a chapter to it (pp. 278–302). Though he does not put it in these words, for Bakhtin eating is like a materialist parody of the Eucharist: 'Here man tastes the world, introduces it into his body, makes it part of himself . . . the act of eating is joyful, triumphant . . .' (p. 281). Feasting makes communal the necessary material principle of ingestion, or the will-to-eat. Nature and society were unified in the cycle of the process of labour, from seed to harvest, earth to table. Complementing this physical and social process was 'the tradition of festive speech' in, for example, the 'grotesque symposium' of Rabelais (pp. 283–4). The anecdotal wit of dinner-party exchange is a distant capitalist mutation of this, though, as we shall see, Bakhtin has some telling asides on the difference between the two. That is, between the public squares of the festive Middle Ages and the private dining rooms and exclusive clubs and hotels of the society of something like *The Importance of Being Earnest* in its preoccupation with dining and witty speech.

The dominant characteristic of Wilde's verbal wit is its carnival inversion. That is to say, in the carnival of the Middle Ages as Bakhtin shows us, social status, propriety and order were reversed by being actually acted out, masters waiting on servants etc. Wilde does this verbally, but his outrageous iconoclasm is doubly subversive since its impulse is from within the ruling class. At the opening of act one, following an exchange concerning his manservant Lane's indifference to a former marriage, Algernon reflects:

> . . . Really, if the lower orders don't set us a good example, what on earth is the use of them? They seem, as a class, to have absolutely no sense of moral responsibility. (p. 322)

Obviously the humour derives from the diametric reversal applied by a member of the upper class from which came, or were supposed to come, examples of social decorum. Algernon then caps this by redirecting his wit from the *hoi polloi* to the Anglican transcendental—'Divorces are made in Heaven' (p. 323). The cosy commonplace giving divine sanction to the

fabric of Victorian society in the sanctity of the family, is given a rude
knock. Algernon is the creator of Mr Bunbury who provides him with
the opportunity for a carnivalesque freedom while seemingly sustaining
the status quo. That is, Algernon appears to be honouring social obli-
gations by ministering to his sick 'friend', while in fact he is taking the
opportunity of avoiding his social commitments to his caste particularly
during the London season. The actual content of his Bunburying, like
that of Jack, his counterpart's adoption of a raffish doppelgänger identity
as Ernest, remains tantalizingly unspecified. Given the comic tenor we
hardly suspect a Dr Jekyll and Mr Hyde situation, but nevertheless critics
have descried a cryptic biographical analogue to Wilde's Bunburying in
the homosexual London underworld.

Wilde, however, does not confine such inversion to his seemingly trans-
gressive characters. That aristocratic pillar of society, Lady Bracknell herself,
becomes the vehicle for witty inversion in a way that seems to reflect the carnivalesque, yet ultimately inverts it, thereby prefiguring the restoration of the
all-encompassing status quo, within and outside the theatre. Interrogating her
prospective son-in-law, a sudden interjection reveals to Lady Bracknell that
Jack is a smoker. The dialectic of inversion which follows is serpentine. Initially, Lady Bracknell's response not only overturns puritanical reprehension
(Carnival versus Lent, a motif we will pick up later) by not censuring indulgence, 'I am glad to hear it' (p. 331), but converts it into its opposite, idleness
to industry, 'A man should always have an occupation. There are far too many
idle men in London as it is' (p. 331). With the ironic comic equivocation on
'occupation' the distinction between the upper class man of leisure and the
working class unemployed is collapsed by a collation of the classes by which
Jack is made an inverted carnival holiday figure of the lower orders in Sunday
best, an image covertly suggested later, by inference that, as a foundling, Jack
might well be a bastard. That is to say, as a temporarily compromised symbol
of carnival inversion, the legitimacy of a whole ruling class is glimpsed as not
organic, ordained and necessary, but quite arbitrary. This inference is seen
quite clearly in what immediately follows in the dialogue.

Lady Bracknell approves of Jack's frank confession of ignorance, an
ignorance which further allies him with the lower classes:

> I am pleased to hear it. I do not approve of anything that tampers
> with natural ignorance ... The whole theory of modern education
> is radically unsound. Fortunately in England, at any rate, education
> produces no effect whatsoever. If it did, it would prove a serious
> danger to the upper classes, and probably lead to acts of violence in
> Grosvenor Square. (pp. 331–2)

The paradoxical logic of the social implications behind the humour is that the only thing that separates the lower and upper classes otherwise united in their 'ignorance', apart from educational reformers, is money. And that is made the immediate topic of the following conversation in which Jack is made to reveal that his country gentleman pose is, in fact, belt on stocks and shares, not on land, much to Lady Bracknell's iconoclastic approval. Bakhtin tells us of the 'parodies and travesties' (p. 11) that were part of carnival and such mockery of both liberal and conservative positions here provides a dizzying pastiche of carnival counterpoint which is ultimately licensed by the form and occasion of the comedy itself.

Elsewhere the wit is shifted from character to character as ventriloquistic vehicles for the author's epigrammatic inversions as it becomes apparent that the carnival reversal shifts from society to art, from the holiday iconoclasm of ethical subversion by the characters, to their creator the carnival king, in effect, the artist himself, Oscar Wilde, who is waited on by his social superiors, the upper class audience present in the St James's theatre. As clown-king Wilde systematically turns upside down the Victorian preoccupation with such things as manners, sincerity and hypocrisy. His dandy surrogates, Algernon and Jack, achieve a relative carnival freedom from social restraint, yet cannot, like Wilde himself, escape the overriding necessity of the importance of being gentlemen. When Algernon Bunburys to Woolton, Jack's country house, to masquerade as Ernest, all-encompassing society nevertheless determines his self-presentation. Lane is to pack ' . . . dress clothes . . . smoking jacket, and all the Bunbury suits . . .' (p. 337) into 'Three portmanteaus, a dressing case [and) two hat boxes' (p. 346). Similarly, whatever Jack-as-Ernest's private or public escape from the constraints of country guardianships he nevertheless maintains a very fashionable gentleman's residence—"Mr Ernest Worthing, B.4, The Albany, W"—as his conventional card proclaims. Society determines behaviour inescapably but wit can apparently surmount convention both informally in life (Wilde as celebrated guest) and formally in art (Wilde as playwright). Moreover, a further challenge to authority and convention at the heart of carnival, and at the heart of Wilde's play, remains to be explored. Namely, the function throughout of eating.

At the beginning of act one an immediate carnivalesque inversion is displaced by something related but infinitely more ramified in the context of the play. Firstly, Algernon remarks that while Lord Shoreham and Jack were recently dining with him, his servant Lane helped himself to the champagne. That is, in carnivalesque egalitarian terms, Lane made himself symbolically equal with his masters. This transgression is duplicated by the wayward Algernon-as-Ernest during Jack's absence from Woolton '—Under an assumed name he drank, I've just been informed by my butler, an entire pint bottle of my Perriet-Jouet, Brut, '89' (p. 363). Algernon's (and it will be shown, Jack's) compulsive eating is reflected against formal social dining throughout the play. As a bourgeois norm dining is the cultivated nexus of social etiquette and intercourse by which classes corroborate their caste hegemony through exchange and permutation, in a kind of capitalist potlatch tokenism. Algernon's Bunburying helps him evade the chore of dining with family in order to dine with Jack 'at Willis's' (p. 326). Part of the inverted wit is most revealing at this point. 'I hate people who are not serious about meals' says Algernon, 'It is so shallow of them' (p. 327). Given the pattern of social and ethical reversal this refers to both food and dining, and the contemporary object of the satire is readily apparent behind Algernon's posture. Yet in a twentieth-century context of sociological and psychoanalytical theory Algernon is hoist by his own petard. At the close of act two Algernon jokingly acknowledges that 'When I am in trouble, eating is the only thing that consoles me' (p. 357): a resonant admission in the post-Freudian world.

Psychoanalytical understanding of compulsive eating as a compensatory sex substitute would seem to be relevant here but the structural implications of a Bakhtinian reading takes us more incisively into the character, the play, and the society. As the play opens, Algernon greedily consumes the cucumber sandwiches he has had especially prepared to give Lady Bracknell tea during her visit. As he defensively responds to Jack's charge 'Eating as usual, I see, Algy!'—'I believe it is customary in good society to take some slight refreshment at five o'clock' (p. 322). Of course it is far from customary to eat the food prepared for a guest. Algy's compulsive eating here accompanies the carnival wit examined above. Thus the affront to society is duplicated in speech and action and the conventions of polite society are subverted—Lady Bracknell has to go without. Algernon's behaviour is repeated at Woolton where he voraciously consumes all the muffins (and that bottle of champagne). Unsurprisingly, included with his Bunburying luggage is 'a luncheon basket' (p. 346).

The original four act version of *The Importance of Being Earnest* included a section known as 'The Gribsby Episode'[4] but this scene was excised from the script submitted to the censorship of the Lord Chamberlain's office. The shorter three-act version has remained the usually preferred choice for performance. Gribsby is a solicitor who arrives at Woolton to serve a court order on 'Ernest' Worthing for unpaid supper bills at the Savoy Hotel, amounting to £762.14.2. There is no indication whether these suppers were like Algernon's solitary gormandising, or in company. Either way Miss Prism is aghast at the 'grossly materialistic', and even Algernon sees it as 'monstrous',[5] terms reminiscent of Bakhtin's carnival grotesque. In these Gargantuan eating habits of Algernon and Jack appetite inverts the manners of social dining and as such might be considered a kind of carnivalesque overturning of society's norms, to some extent. Yet there are crucial differences as well as likenesses. As noted above, Wilde aligns the carnivalesque activities of eating and humour, which Bakhtin discusses, yet elsewhere Bakhtin stresses the communal aspect of feasting, not the solitary gluttony of an Algernon and (possibly) Jack. Again Bakhtin stresses that in the carnivalesque world of the grotesque body 'Man's encounter with the world in the act of eating is joyful, triumphant' (p. 281). With Algernon and Jack it is apologetic and almost illicit. Further, for Bakhtin 'the image of food often symbolized the entire labor process' (p. 281). Evidently, in *The Importance of Being Earnest* all food symbolizes the class distinction and separation of capitalist bourgeois society and the fissiparous distinctions of fashion within it. Gwendolyn the town sophisticate '*superciliously*' puts down Cecily the country ward—'Sugar is not fashionable' (p. 353). At one point Bakhtin offers an appropriate general comment which may be applied to Algernon and Jack and all that they represent:

> . . . images in the popular festive tradition . . . differ sharply from the images of private eating or private gluttony and drunkenness in early bourgeois literature. The latter express the contentment and satiety of the selfish individual, his personal enjoyment, and not the triumph of the people as a whole. (pp. 301–2)

This apparent carnival in Wilde's play, which upon re-examination can be seen to be a complex interaction of carnival and anti-carnival, is like a structural unconformity or, in organic terms, a genetic throwback. Two crucial instances particularly bring this out, both concerning anecdotes of Lady Harbury, as follows:

LADY BRACKNELL: . . . I was obliged to call on dear Lady Harbury. I hadn't been there since her poor husband's death. I never saw a woman so altered: she looks quite twenty years younger. And now I'll have a cup of tea, and one of those nice cucumber sandwiches you promised me. (p. 327).

LADY BRACKNELL: . . . I had some crumpets with Lady Harbury, who seems to me to be living entirely for pleasure now.

ALGERNON: I hear her hair has turned quite gold from grief. (p. 328)

To be noted here is the collocation of humour, eating, death and rejuvenation. In the festive world of carnival culture death and earth both devour, but giving new birth. Eating is an analogous symbolic process. All centre on

Bakhtin's concept of 'degradation' (the higher to the lower, the transcendental to the material) in which birth and death, age and youth, copulation and
defecation are complementary, not polarities (see particularly pp. 20–1). But
unlike carnival humour, Wilde's satire here recalls Bakhtin's differentiation
between folk grotesque and capitalist facetiousness:

> The satirist whose laughter is negative places himself above
> the object of his mockery, he is opposed to it ... The people's
> ambivalent laughter, on the other hand, expresses the point of view
> of the whole world; he who is laughing also belongs to it. (p. 12)

Paradoxically, the juvenescence of birth and rebirth in *The Importance of
Being Earnest* is reversed and becomes sterility and a form of death. Either
mistakenly or facetiously Canon Chasuble refers to Miss Prism as Egeria:
she reminds him that Laetitia is her actual name. The mockery of Laetitia
for someone professionally obliged to maidenhood is evident but Chasuble's
slip is quite pointed by Wilde. Egeria, or Aegeria, was one of the Roman
Camenae, or prophetic nymphs, and was a giver of life often invoked by
pregnant women. Chasuble is himself a declared celibate, and Miss Prism
identifies the mark left by a 'temperance beverage' (p. 367) in the notorious
handbag. Clearly these two represent the repressive and abstemious Lenten
aspect of Victorian life, within the play, in contrast to the vestigial carnival
in the presentation of Algernon and Jack. However, even the latter pair
undergo the antithesis of carnival death-birth in a travestied birth-death in
the sacraments of Anglicanism by which the play's closure of comedic marriage may be seen, from a carnival perspective, as a metaphorical death in
society's reclamation.

Carnival laughs at death. As Bakhtin puts it, 'the medieval and Renaissance grotesque, filled with the spirit of carnival, liberates the world from
all that is dark and terrifying; it takes away all fears and is therefore completely gay and bright' (p. 47). Thus the grotesque of death and laughter which
indeed survives in Wilde's play. Jack appears as the figure of death, '*Enter
JACK slowly from the back of the garden. He is dressed in the deepest mourning,
the crepe hatband and black gloves*' (p. 342). Jack is in mourning for 'Ernest'
who has to be killed off. Similarly 'Mr Bunbury' is finally made to succumb
by Algernon. That is, the means of carnival for Jack and Algernon have to
be sacrificed as they prepare to re-enter society fulfilling the pattern of Sat-
urnalian closure. In the medieval world of carnival death rejuvenates by rebirth. Here the literal christening pursued by Jack and Algernon symbolises
a conformist christening into Victorian earnestness, assisted by that bastion
of the Anglican establishment, Dr Chasuble. Social legitimacy and comedic

decorum coincide to determine Jack's actual rebirth as Ernest indeed, to be married, along with Algernon, into the world they had sought to escape by carnival, in words and actions.

The theatre of the 1890s restored an upper-class comedy of manners after the dominance of decades of music-hall populism. In every sense Wilde's wit was licensed, and he above all was the licensed Lord of Misrule, clown-king of carnival in his life and in his art of comedy. The painter Whistler once expostulated with the public dandy and aesthete, 'What means this unseemly carnival . . . ?'[6] In the fulness of time the meaning became apparent as Wilde's Saturnalia came to an end. 'Ernest' and 'Mr Bunbury' were killed off and then *The Importance of Being Earnest* itself had to be closed because of Wilde's notoriety. Bakhtin and many other commentators on carnival fail to mention that in the early forms of the festival the King of Saturnalia was dethroned and then sacrificed.[7] And so Wilde had to propitiate the Lenten gods of Victorian society.

Staged inversion could be celebrated but sexual inversion in life could not be tolerated. In 'The Gribsby Episode' Holloway prison is threatened and that is indeed where Wilde was imprisoned on remand before his sentence of two years hard labour. In *The Importance of Being Earnest* Jack says that Ernest 'seems to have expressed a desire to be buried in Paris' (p. 343), where in fact Wilde was interred. If, that is, the comic spirit can ever be laid to rest.

Notes

1. G.F. Maine (ed.) *The Works of Oscar Wilde* (London, 1963), p. 356. All references are to this edition.

2. Cam. Mass. 1964. All references are to this edition.

3. Albert Grenier *The Roman Spirit in Religion, Thought and Art* (London, 1926), p. 89.

4. Joseph Bristow (ed) *The Importance of Being Earnest and Related Writings* (London, 1992), pp. 88–94.

5. Op. cit., p. 91.

6. Richard Ellmann *Oscar Wilde* (London, 1988), p. 147.

7. Grenier *loc. cit.* and see Mircea Eliade (ed) *The Encyclopedia of Religion* (New York, 1987), vol. 3, p. 98.

MICHAEL PATRICK GILLESPIE

The Victorian Impulse in Contemporary Audiences: The Regularization of The Importance of Being Earnest

From its first performance on Valentine's Day 1895 to the present, a marvelous imaginative variety has characterized the stage interpretations of *The Importance of Being Earnest*. At the same time, as one saw in the 1993 West End performance featuring Maggie Smith's portrayal of Lady Bracknell as a woman whose domineering manner only partially masks her *nouvelle venue* insecurities, directors over the years have generally approached the play from a particular artistic point of view that sets the tone for its stage interpretation.[1] Still, the rich range of perspectives adopted by various productions attests to a significant creative achievement: Wilde's most successful effort at playwriting brings into equilibrium all the distinct formal and thematic elements he developed with varying degrees of success in his social melodramas written earlier in the decade, and it allows performance of the play from a number of equally valid points of view. Unfortunately, despite the play's combination of familiarity and innovation, established through gestures aiming toward integration rather than displacement, particular productions of *The Importance of Being Earnest* often fail to address fully the play's pluralistic scope.

The same condition has characterized many critical assessments of the play. The wealth of diverse material amalgamated into the discourse of *The Importance of Being Earnest* has always provoked strong interpretive responses,

From *Oscar Wilde and the Poetics of Ambiguity*, pp. 100–14, 184–85. Copyright © 1996 by the Board of Regents of the State of Florida.

55

particularly over the course of the past two decades. Scholars sensitive to these concerns have offered illuminating new readings by foregrounding topics long ignored.[2] At the same time, literary critics—like directors of theatrical productions—have tended to enforce their interpretations by focusing on selected distinguishing features that support a specific central concern without extending full consideration to the play's pluralistic potential.[3]

A number of recent studies, for example, have employed rhetorical patterns of interpretation to draw attention to the playful manipulation of language that runs throughout the dialogue.[4] Taking a cue from the dualistic word play encapsuled in the title's Ernest/Earnest pun, these interpretations offer readings based upon the transposition of overt and implicit signification. In effect, they examine Wilde's use of irony to facilitate the movement away from the conventional certitude that characterizes most melodrama. These approaches certainly provide useful perspectives for seeing *The Importance of Being Earnest*, but they often presume a linguistic stability that the twists of the play's discourse deny. If taken no further, such methods can lapse into binary, either/or viewpoints that truncate the imaginative process suggested by the playfulness running through the drama.

I advocate a response more suited to the mutability of Wilde's language, one that exploits the ambivalence of the title by incorporating pluralism into one's initial linguistic response in a way that underscores the play's self-conscious ambiguity. This means, for example, allowing for the possibility that the past participle "Being" in the title could be synonymous with both "Seeming" and "Becoming." The protean condition, of course, comes out of Nietzsche's now familiar juxtaposition. Roland Barthes, as part of an effort to form "a theory of materialist subject," reminds us of the conjunction of text, pleasure, and bliss with the following quotation from Nietzsche: "We have no right to ask *who* it is who interprets. It is interpretation itself, a form of the will to power, which exists (not as 'being' but as process, a becoming) as passion."[5] This method would, by extension, make one aware of a polyphony within the adjective *Earnest* that goes well beyond the binary limits of double entendre through its evocation of the uncommon noun *Ernest*.

Following this mode of interpretation, one sees that the title of the play expands the scope of Earnest/Ernest and suggests a more flexible mode of addressing cruxes within the discourse. (The subtitle, "A Trivial Comedy for Serious People," similarly fosters such an approach.) By introducing this sense of the multiplicity within the discourse of the drama, the title disposes one toward pluralism and forestalls truncated responses. Under these protocols, for example, Cecily Cardew's ability to fabricate a wonderful image of Ernest that both conforms to and circumvents the limitations of a conventional courtship becomes more than a piece of melodramatic silliness.

CECILY. And this is the box in which I keep all your dear letters. [*Kneels at table, opens box, and produces letters tied up with blue ribbon.*]

ALGERNON. My letters! But my own sweet Cecily, I have never written you any letters.

CECILY. You need hardly remind me of that, Ernest. I remember only too well that I was forced to write your letters for you. I always wrote three times a week, and sometimes oftener.

ALGERNON. Oh, do let me read them, Cecily?

CECILY. Oh, I couldn't possibly. They would make you far too conceited. [*Replaces box.*] The three you wrote me after I had broken off the engagement are so beautiful, and so badly spelled, that even now I can hardly read them without crying a little. (*Writings*, 513)

With deft, unself-conscious expressiveness, Cecily first announces her arrogation of the roles of both author and audience and then goes on to demonstrate her powers as a writer and her sensitivity as a reader. More to the point, over the course of her remarks, she represents for us the way that characters within the play routinely function on multiple levels. At the same time, through her actions she offers us a model for responding to *The Importance of Being Earnest* as writerly readers.

This multifaceted aestheticism that I am advocating in readings of *The Picture of Dorian Gray*, *The Importance of Being Earnest*, and other works by Wilde gives rise to the same ambiguity that characterizes a larger interpretive trend toward the amalgamation of diverse analytical views. Critics commonly bring together ideas derived from very different approaches (such as feminism and deconstruction or Marxism and psychoanalysis) into single readings held together by a common interpretive lexicon. At the same time, any specific term addresses a range of meanings and consequently avoids the danger of imposing prescriptive language on our readings. Thus, our use of concepts such as Victorianism, Modernism, and post-Modernism insistently asserts the interpretive power that comes out of common yet adaptable terminology.[6]

By uniting a group of loosely related characteristics under a single designation, each label contributes to the constitution of a shared vocabulary for readers with a variety of backgrounds. These classifications impart a broad sense of the interpretive perspectives held by the critics employing them without limiting their application to rigidly narrow designations. Imaginative resonances result, despite the diverse attitudes of those involved, because the terms *Victorianism*, *Modernism*, and *post-Modernism* do not function simply as artificially imposed parameters. Rather, like the words *author* and *reader*, they encapsulate concerns constituent to any number of disparate methodologies without immediately privileging a narrow representation of any term or a strict delineation of a particular approach.

These benefits, of course, do not accrue only to analyses that single out the periods designated by the three terms I have just cited. Critics with approaches as different as those of A. C. Bradley and Stephen Greenblatt have offered sharply different responses that show the interpretive advantage that one derives by remaining attentive to various elements of the social repertoire of sixteenth-century England as manifested in Shakespeare's plays. Further, both have demonstrated that recognizing the influence of culturally defined material (united by the label *Renaissance*) on the creation of art allows a reader to appreciate the delicate balance between specific intra- and extratextual forces that contribute to an aesthetic experience. Nonetheless, and this feature distinguishes such terms from those found in the hermeneutics of ideologically deterministic criticism, the ability to sustain widespread and varied applications brings out the protean interpretive alternatives in concepts like Renaissance without isolating diverse perspectives from one another.

E. M. W. Tillyard, as he outlined the society of *The Elizabethan World Picture*, found the need to stretch the frame not just to accommodate the late Tudor/early Stuart age of Shakespeare and Donne but also to include the interregnum period of Milton. Whether this occurred because Tillyard had a greater sense than others of the era's boundaries or because he had a tolerance for flexibility belied by the title of his book makes little difference. His own semantic suppleness and the resulting stimulation in critical thinking brought about by concepts outlined by his work show the force of such terms. Critics found Tillyard's designation neither totally acceptable nor completely incomprehensible. Rather, they viewed it as outlining a set of assumptions characterizing significant topics for discussion, but only in an approximate fashion that defined a common ground of interest while stimulating diverse responses. The value of this label—and of others like it—over ideologically deterministic terms obtains as long as it maintains a flexibility that resists prescriptive applications.[7]

An examination of the way that readers conventionally apply these chronological terms illustrates our predisposition toward multiplicity and supports the argument that I am advancing for interpreting *The Importance of Being Earnest*. While we use labels such as *Victorian, Modern*, or *post-Modern* in a shorthand fashion to sum up the attitudes associated with a particular historical era, we feel no constraint to restrict such applications chronologically. On the contrary, a sizable body of critical work evinces a willingness to discover Victorian, Modern, and post-Modern tendencies in writings from the earliest periods to the present, underscoring an interpretive latitude that counteracts such monolithic inclinations.[8]

Naturally enough, when one brings post-Modern sensibilities formed out of a Modernist tradition to bear upon a Victorian work, conflicting values assert themselves. Reconciling the polyphony resulting from these conflicting views provides a paradigm for dealing with the pluralism throughout Wilde's play, for it underscores the hypostatic interpretive ambiance that *The Importance of Being Earnest* fosters: describing the play against a backdrop of Victorianism; recognizing the Modernist inclinations to privilege individual perspectives; and acknowledging the post-Modern assumptions that any contemporary reader will bring to its discourse. Thus, while *The Importance of Being Earnest* repeatedly evokes specific conventions that can enhance one's comprehension, its continual disruption of expectations encourages us to resist closure and adopt a pluralistic approach. One sees this exemplified in the diverse representations of the figure of Ernest that appear throughout the play.

Ernest exists as a different individual in the imaginations of each of the play's central characters, in much the same fashion as images of Dorian Gray exist in the imaginations of the novel's principal characters. Unlike concepts of Dorian that one finds in *The Picture of Dorian Gray*, however, readers of *The Importance of Being Earnest* need not limit their imaginative constructions of Ernest to the impressions generated by a specific figure within the work, as they must when conceptualizing Dorian Gray. Consequently, the referentiality that surrounds concepts of Dorian (discussed in chapter 3) does not impose a form of closure upon our interpretations of the Ernests that we encounter. In fact, from the start of Wilde's drama, each of the Ernests brought into existence by the diverse imaginations of Jack, Algy, Cecily, and Gwendolen clearly lacks the substance to enforce his dominance as a definitive concept. As a result, the reader forms his or her discrete sense of Ernest from an amalgamation and a reconstitution of all these evocations.

The implications of this response go well beyond the simplistic idea that each of us interprets words differently and that anyone can justify the exclusivity of a particular reading through the easy application of the term *provisional*. The Ernests that abound in the play affirm the pluralistic concept that a range of cultural influences produce the potential for simultaneously maintaining a variety of equally probable meanings from the same discourse. As a result, one can identify at any given point in the drama numerous possible interpretations of Ernest competing for recognition without feeling a concurrent necessity to select one in preference to all the others.

The entire structure of *The Importance of Being Earnest* rests upon diverse and often contradictory points of view, and the witty dialogue of its characters continually reinforces the complexity of that condition. As Algy notes, "[t]he truth is rarely pure and never simple. Modern life would be very tedious if it were either, and modern literature a complete impossibility" (*Writings*, 485). Any interpretation that circumscribes the play's imaginative breadth by excluding multiple alternatives from simultaneous consideration would find itself operating outside the work's own epistemological parameters.

This may seem a rather nebulous interpretive charge; but as demonstrated by the scene (quoted previously) that outlines Cecily Cardew's skills as both writer and reader, the formal structure of *The Importance of Being Earnest* does offer broad intratextual guidance for developing a pluralistic approach. Over the course of the play, one finds that each of the play's four central characters places a great deal of importance upon someone being Ernest, yet their perfectly earnest (albeit solipsistic) individual attitudes attach a range of equally plausible significations to that signifier. For Algernon Moncrieff, Ernest is simply his friend Jack Worthing: "You have always told me that [your name] was Ernest. I have introduced you to every one as Ernest. You answer to the name of Ernest. You look as if your name was Ernest. You are the most earnest-looking person I ever saw in my life. It is perfectly absurd your saying that your name isn't Ernest. It's on your cards" (*Writings*, 484). For Jack Worthing, on the other hand, Ernest represents a displacement of imagination and desire, "a younger brother . . . who lives in the Albany, and gets into the most dreadful scrapes" (*Writings*, 485). For Gwendolen Fairfax, Ernest appears as a moral and ethical paragon, "a strong upright Nature. He is the very soul of truth and honour. Disloyalty would be as impossible to him as deception" (*Writings*, 517). And for Cecily Cardew, Ernest is the romantic creature growing out of her conversations with Miss Prism: "And of course a man who is much talked about is always very attractive" (*Writings*, 513).

Ultimately, the discourse leaves the reconciliation of these diverse perceptions to the reader; for despite the attention lavished upon the figure of Ernest, nothing near a consensus emerges as to what or whom the word represents to the individuals on stage. Instead, while the intensity of the importance given to that designation remains constant, its nature varies wildly from character to character. In part, at least, this disparity arises from the fact that, although an aura of exquisiteness informs the dialogue throughout the play, no two individuals seem to speak exactly the same language. Certainly, no two characters draw precisely the same significance or signification from the vocabularies that they employ. (This situation embodies the Victorian, Modern, post-Modern formulation examined earlier. No two people give precisely the same meaning to any of these words, yet we all think that we understand what someone else means who uses the terms.)

As one might expect, such conditions foster strikingly different points of view among the central characters. Nonetheless, a remarkable openness to diversity of meaning pervades the discourse. Nearly everyone tolerates a widespread and casual application of a range of idiosyncratically constituted expressions. Because of this tolerance, much of the drama's humor relies directly upon the audience's cognizance of so many characters speaking at cross-purposes.

Employing these formulaic misperceptions invokes a technique that has served as a comedic standby since the age of Aristophanes, but Wilde's application interposes a sophisticated variation upon the usual routine. As one can see from the following remarks by Jack and Algy, miscommunications do not occur because of stock physical impairments or predictable intellectual differences. Characters simply refuse to concern themselves with the rendering of a term in any fashion other than the one that they themselves have settled upon.

JACK. Oh, Gwendolen is as right as a trivet. As far as she is concerned we are engaged. Her mother is perfectly unbearable. Never met such a Gorgon . . . I don't really know what a Gorgon is like, but I am quite sure that Lady Bracknell is one. In any case, she is a monster, without being a myth, which is rather unfair . . . I beg your pardon, Algy, I suppose I shouldn't talk about your own aunt in that way before you.

ALGERNON. My dear boy, I love hearing my relations abused. It is the only thing that makes me put up with them at all. Relations are simply a tedious pack of people, who haven't got the remotest knowledge of how to live, nor the smallest instinct about when to die.

JACK. Oh, that is nonsense!

ALGERNON. It isn't!

JACK. Well, I won't argue about the matter. You always want to argue about things.

ALGERNON. That is exactly what things were originally made for.

JACK. Upon my word, if I thought that I'd shoot myself . . . (A pause.) You don't think there is any chance of Gwendolen becoming like her mother in about a hundred and fifty years, do you Algy?

ALGERNON. All women become like their mothers. That is their tragedy. No man does. That is his. (*Writings*, 496) [author's ellipsis]

Precisely this type of exchange, representative of a pattern recurring throughout the play, demonstrates to readers the discourse's determination to discourage interpretations based upon linear, exclusionary methodologies.

Its insistent depictions of the suppleness of language take the form of a range of enthusiastically self-contradictory points of view that serve as the basis for the play's humor: Although individuals repeatedly find themselves at odds with the ways that others use common terms, no one feels the need to regularize the situation. The equanimity of Wilde's characters in turn provides his audience with a model for deriving meaning that allows us to proceed without disrupting the continuity of the various discourses. Instead, one balances all exchanges around apprehensions of a series of analogous, but not identical, meanings.

The kinetic nature of drama, of course, has already prepared us for just such an interpretive maneuver, for even the most putatively prescriptive play cannot relegate the audience to a completely static role. The very act of viewing leads one to reconstitute the play that one sees. Whatever perspective one adopts—choosing to center attention on one actor rather than upon the interplay of dialogues unfolding before us, or attending to the dramatic abilities of the cast rather than focusing on plot development, or taking in the costumes and scenery rather than the action on stage—gives one an active part in creating meaning.

The Importance of Being Earnest functions on even more complex aesthetic levels. As it first invites and then frustrates traditional expectations, the play clearly encourages its audience to accommodate multiplicity when moving through the various stages of apprehension that one experiences. The whole concept of the range of views of Ernest wonderfully illustrates this point. The oscillation among different perspectives leads readers toward increasingly radical efforts to impose order upon the aesthetic sensations that the work arouses.

Although Wilde's intentions do not directly affect the approach to reading that I am suggesting, evidence indicates that he certainly wished to underscore the importance of maintaining rather than resolving the tension between conventionality and unconventionality. In his biography of Wilde, Richard Ellmann has transcribed notes from Max Beerbohm's copy of *The Importance of Being Earnest* that offer additional support for my views:

> [Beerbohm's] copy contained two restorations based upon his memory of the first performance, which Wilde had forgotten: at the end of Act I, Jack says, "Oh, that's nonsense, Algy, you never talk anything but nonsense," to which Algernon replies, "Nobody every does." Beerbohm says the speech should go on, "And besides, I *love* nonsense." He also corrected Miss Prism's words to Cecily in Act II: "The chapter on the Fall of the Rupee you may omit. It is somewhat too sensational. Even these metallic problems have

their melodramatic side." Beerbohm preferred to this last sentence [*sic*] what he remembered from the original, "It is somewhat too unconventional for a young girl."[9]

Whether these emendations represent accurate restorations of Wilde's original dialogue remains moot. In terms of my argument, however, the case with which Beerbohm fit them into his own text enforces the validity of that the play lends itself to such imaginative responses from its readers.

To return to a position articulated earlier in the chapter: An exclusive reliance upon cultural, ideological, or generic conventions can have a catalytic effect upon one's reading. Nonetheless, when such a methodology does not fully develop the interpretive potential of the play, an audience begins to feel restive. However one attempts to take seriously the triviality of Wilde's drama, features contradicting such a single-minded approach continually obtrude upon one's perceptions. The whole question of identity, as the play considers it, illustrates my point; and in the remaining pages of this chapter I will use it to outline hermeneutic questions that I will address in greater detail in chapter 6.

Given the seeming priggishness of Jack and the apparent silliness of Algy, one might at first accept the need for Jack to create a nonexistent brother (Ernest) and for Algy to invent an equally fictitious friend (Bunbury) as a source of harmless fun. Expectations about the way that a playwright structures this type of domestic comedy reinforce such an assumption. As the play develops, however, the complexity of their deceptions invites one to look for more specific motivations; and one begins to consider the possibility that their trips to London or the country involve embarking upon the sort of behavior that they do not wish to be readily linked to their own names. In fact, their emphatic need for the secrecy surrounding their behavior away from home invites the supposition that both Jack and Algy lead at the very least irregular and very likely debauched lives.

The discourse of the play never resolves the ambiguity over the creation of false identities, so viewers maintain a multiple sense of these two characters that one might designate as inclusively innocent, corrupt, and amoral—or, to assign different values to these three perspectives, simultaneously Victorian, Modern, and post-Modern in their outlooks.[10] The play's representations of Jack and Algy can easily sustain these diverse features because these attitudes both play upon and undermine the audience's inclinations to use archetypes and even stereotypes as a basis for forming unified impressions. The behavior of Jack and Algy continually strains our capacity to reconcile their specific natures to the dramatic types that seem to have served as the basis of their personalities, for the two young men evoke familiar theatrical conventions yet hint at far richer characterizations than characters in farces can usually sustain.

Just as the principal male characters of *The Importance of Being Earnest* insinuate more than they reveal, leaving it to the viewers to fill in the gaps, the female figures in the play present additional features that further disrupt conventional interpretive associations. The women, in fact, create even more ambiguity and—in terms of societal norms—aberrance than do the men. They combine behavior that provokes pluralistic perspectives with interpretations of their own that foster multiplicity.

On one hand, Gwendolen and Cecily embody the most noble aspects of social rectitude by virtue of their unswerving determination to employ particular and exacting standards for choosing their prospective husbands, an exquisite refinement of the principal of exclusivity. At the same time, the conditions (centered on the name Ernest) that each lays down for a suitor to meet veer as far from the cultural norms of the period as do the social attitudes embraced by the young men whom they select. (One need only contrast the self-assured views of either woman with the tortured self-interrogations of Henry James's Isabel Archer or George Eliot's Dorothea Brooke to see the enormity of the difference.) Paradoxically, however, even as their independent behavior marks them as unique to this genre, by the very assertion of that independence—setting the name Ernest as a prerequisite for acceptance—they assume the traditional roles of blocking figures with as much vigor and determination as Lady Bracknell displays.

This oscillation encourages one to set aside any inclinations to interpret the plan according to conventional expectations. From the start, these female figures read the world differently and in consequence assert idiosyncrasies that vigorously strain against the bonds of predictable archetypal patterning:

ALGERNON. (To GWENDOLEN.) Dear me, you are smart!
GWENDOLEN. I am always smart! Am I not, Mr Worthing?
JACK. You're quite perfect, Miss Fairfax.
GWENDOLEN. Oh! I hope I am not that. It would leave no room to develop-
    ments, and I intend to develop in many directions. (*Writings*, 487–88)

Gwendolen's easy responses to Algernon and Jack do more than keep them off balance. Her repartee challenges all who wish to interpret her performance. She gives us a sense of her awareness of the conventions characterizing the pert behavior of girls like her in plays like this: "I am always smart! Am I not, Mr Worthing?" But in rejecting Jack's elaboration of the epithet, she refuses either to accept the full conventions of the role or to define an alternative that she would embrace. Rather, she maintains an openness to possibilities—"I intend to develop in many directions"—and draws the audience into both/and speculations upon her nature.

Other female characters embrace similarly pluralistic roles. Lady Bracknell, for example, implicitly defines herself as a paragon of public virtue with precise ideas regarding the societal criteria that her daughter's prospective suitors must meet before being judged suitable. At the same time, like Gwendolen, she habitually maintains only the most tenuous links between her views and common social customs. In fact, whenever there arises a conflict between personal values and communal mores, conventions always give way to Lady Bracknell's own idiosyncratic ideas. Her interrogations of Jack Worthing (*Writings*, 492–95), discussed in greater detail in chapter 6, amply illustrate this point.

The Importance of Being Earnest supports this studied irregularity in its presentation of minor characters. Miss Prism, for example, also moves according to an idiosyncratic vision that runs counter to general practice. Her complete self-involvement, evinced through her absent-minded abandonment of the infant Jack/Ernest in Victoria Station and more recently in her haphazard supervision of Cecily, gives ample evidence of an inclination to adhere to public standards only in a highly subjective fashion that conforms to her own interests. Societal mores never inhibit her behavior. Rather, they provide the means to justify and expedite actions that she has already decided to pursue.

MISS PRISM. I think, dear Doctor, I will have a stroll with you. I find I have a headache after all, and a walk might do it good.
CHASUBLE. With pleasure, Miss Prism, with pleasure. We might go as far as the schools and back.
MISS PRISM. That would be delightful. Cecily, you will read your Political Economy in my absence. The chapter on the Fall of the Rupee you may omit. It is somewhat too sensational. Even these metallic problems have their melodramatic side. (*Writings*, 502)

Even the Reverend Chasuble—although not as adept as the women in the play—allows himself such a flexible conception of his duties as an Anglican priest that he can schedule and reschedule the christenings of Jack and Algy with little or no apparent thought to the significance of the event (*Writings*, 507–8). Some may feel uneasy at giving so much interpretive weight to rather mundane events. That, however, is exactly what Wilde has invited us to do in the subtitle of his play: simultaneously recognize the play's seriousness and its triviality.

Admittedly, balancing the degree of trifling and weighty responses that one derives from any reading of *The Importance of Being Earnest* requires a measure of dexterity. Christopher Nassaar's study of Wilde's works shows how one can run into difficulty by failing to maintain his equilibrium. Nassaar has adroitly taken note of the secret lives of Jack and Algy; but he has also minimized the implications by viewing their behavior as a broad parody of the life of Dorian Gray, endorsing the reductive reading of the characters as nothing more than innocent, harmless, and frivolous children.[11] One can still, of course, enjoy the work from that perspective, but such a view does not begin to exhaust the full interpretive potential of *The Importance of Being Earnest*.

Inevitably the discourse creates situations that make the imposition of the sort of resolution that Nassaar advocates too artificial and inhibiting for the reader to accept. While the play ostensibly invokes the world of Victorian melodrama where figures fit neatly into either/or classifications, it simultaneously resists efforts to subsume all implications of guilt and scandal within a broad and easy acceptance of appearances. Like Steven Marcus's "other Victorians," the individuals in the play as well as the audience contend with behavioral traits that demand recognition but resist easy integration into the nature of linearly defined characters. As I have already noted, one cannot resolve this condition by means of a simple inversion—replacing the old (heterosexual) morality with a new (homosexual) one.

In fact, to return to a concept touched upon earlier in the chapter, cultural oscillation causes Modern and post-Modern impulses repeatedly to insinuate themselves into texts of Wilde's Victorian drama. This alternative produces conflicting attitudes and feelings, and that ambivalence exerts a shaping aesthetic influence on the drama. When, for example, we speculate on the nature of Jack's and Algy's secret lives while simultaneously defining their public roles, our response acknowledges that, despite obvious antipathies, conventions describing one set of identities do not negate or even temporarily displace any other.

This pluralistic guideline delineates a useful perspective when the action of the play foregrounds ambiguities. The engagements of Jack and Gwendolen and Algy and Cecily raise immediate questions about what men and women want from marriage. Sex and power seem the most obvious goals; but the framework of *The Importance of Being Earnest*, while not rejecting these motives out of hand, promotes a deferral of the kind of closure that simply accepting them would bring. Because Jack and Algy already have secret lives, marriage would presumably need to offer greater inducements than whatever pleasures they can already enjoy clandestinely. Because Gwendolen and Cecily already exercise a measure of authority over Jack and Algy, the desirability of taking on the burden of a spouse seems problematic at best.

In both cases, of course, the individuals involved cannot openly satisfy their appetites, so embracing roles in which society sanctions sexual gratification and the domination of one's spouse may have particular attractions. Other motivations, however, although initially less obvious, could provide equally likely explanations. Marriage admittedly would do little to increase the power that Gwendolen or Cecily already enjoy, but under the dispensation provided by their status as wives it would make available to them carnal satisfaction (presumably both licit and illicit should they so choose) previously denied.

Likewise, while marriage poses an obvious threat (perhaps not in frequency but certainly in variety) to the opportunities that Jack and Algy have for physical gratification, it would enable them to assume, at least publicly, positions of power and responsibility. Jack already has a measure of this, but only in the fractured form of his country persona. When married, both he and Algy could assume the role of Victorian pater familias. Of course, these combinations would, if anything, make the position of each character more ambiguous; so striving to settle into the regularizing routine of matrimony paradoxically suggests an impulse to replace a modicum of order with added uncertainty.

On a more elemental level, even when motives for marriage predictably feature sexual drives, Wilde's play undermines their conventionality by presenting them as highly disruptive and unstable forces. In this instance, Miss Prism and the Reverend Chasuble, unlike the younger couples, seem single-minded in their quest for physical satisfaction. Age has apparently led to an increase of their sexual appetites, and their energy offers an additional gloss on the play's title. It insinuates earnestness—that is, a determination to pursue one's aims no matter what the cost or difficulty—as a central element of sexual desire. At the same time, the title suggests the pursuit of respectability. Thus, a paradox emerges when it becomes evident that marriage for them would be a source of shame, for it would amount to an open declaration of sexual desire.

CHASUBLE. Were I fortunate enough to be Miss Prism's pupil, I would hang upon her lips. [*Miss Prism glares.*] I spoke metaphorically.—My metaphor was drawn from bees.

* * * * *

MISS PRISM. [*Sententiously.*] And you do not seem to realize, dear Doctor, that by persistently remaining single, a man converts himself into a permanent public temptation. Men should be more careful; this very celibacy leads weaker vessels astray.

CHASUBLE. But is a man not equally attractive when married?

MISS PRISM. No married man is ever attractive except to his wife.
CHASUBLE. And often, I've been told, not even to her.
MISS PRISM. That depends on the intellectual sympathies of the woman.
Maturity can always be depended on. Ripeness can be trusted. Young
women are green. [*Dr. Chasuble starts.*] I spoke horticulturally. My
metaphor was drawn from fruits. (*Writings*, 502, 505)

To return to the analogy, suggested in chapter 4, between Wilde's social
comedies and Restoration drama: Individuals in both groups of plays operate
under the similar influences of multiple and conflicting attitudes. As a result,
like any of the characters in the works of Etherege, Congreve, or Wycherley,
standards completely at odds with conventional mores govern the behavior of
all the individuals in *The Importance of Being Earnest*. Wilde's audience must
struggle through such solipsism and integrate it into the drama's milieu to
gain a full sense of the decorum that regulates the society of the play.

Algy, Jack, and all the others in *The Importance of Being Earnest* stand,
with their reformation of social institutions and perfect amour-propre, in
Victorian garb vacillating between Modernism and post-Modernism. Thus,
we see the order and the disorder of the play not inherently bound to its
thematic content or generational values but coming out of the dramatic text
created by the imaginations of the play's viewers. While one must remain
attentive to the traditional social conventions acting within the work, one
must also acknowledge the functions of alternative social forces. In chapter
6, I will specifically explore how a more precise understanding of the features characterizing a familiar character—the dandy—allows us to derive an
interpretive model that both accommodates ambiguity and offers a coherent
response to the play.

NOTES

1. For a detailed and thoughtful analysis of recent productions, see Robert
Gordon, "Wilde's 'Plays of Modern Life' on the British Stage, 1980–1993," in San-
dulescu, *Rediscovering Wilde*, 156–66.
2. Compare, for instance, Regenia Gagnier, *Idylls of the Marketplace: Oscar
Wilde and the Victorian Public*; Camille A. Paglia, "Oscar Wilde and the English
Epicene"; Christopher Craft, "Alias Bunbury: Desire and Termination in The
Importance of Being Earnest"; Jonathan Dollimore, "Different Desires: Subjectiv-
ity and Transgression in Wilde and Gide"; and Joel Fineman, "The Significance of
Literature: *The Importance of Being Earnest*."
3. Although *The Importance of Being Earnest* has been widely acclaimed,
several prominent critics have attacked it. George Bernard Shaw called the play
"heartless," Arnold Bennett lamented its lack of "the elements of presence," and
Mary McCarthy saw it as completely depraved. Shaw is quoted in Frank Harris,
The Life and Confession of Oscar Wilde, 349. See also his review, reprinted in Karl

Beckson, ed., *Oscar Wilde: The Critical Heritage*, 194–95. The Bennett and McCarthy responses are quoted in Alan Bird, *The Plays of Oscar Wilde*, 181.

4. Compare Paglia, "Oscar Wilde and the English Epicene"; Fineman, "The Significance of Literature"; and Craft, "Alias Bunbury."

5. Roland Barthes, *The Pleasure of the Text*, 61–62, his emphasis. Eve Kosofsky Sedgwick has explored the way that Wilde illuminates Nietzsche in her essay "Some Binarisms (II): Wilde, Nietzsche, and the Sentimental Relations of the Male Body," in *Epistemology of the Closet*, 131–81.

6. For a range of views on Modernism see Malcolm Bradbury and James McFarlane, eds., *Modernism: 1890–1930*; Paul Fussell, *The Great War and Modern Memory*; and Hugh Kenner, *The Pound Era*; Michael Levenson, *A Genealogy of Modernism: A Study of English Literary Doctrine, 1908–1922*. A growing number of critics have begun to address the problematic qualities inherent in terms such as Modernism and post-Modernism. Vincent P. Pecora has surveyed the views central to this debate in his essay "Simulacral Economies." Paradoxically, while criticizing others, Pecora cannot overcome his own nostalgia for these terms, which is perhaps indicative of a larger epistemological problem than he is able to recognize.

7. A. C. Bradley, *Shakespearean Tragedy*; Stephen Greenblatt, *Shakespearean Negotiations: The Circulation of Social Energy in Renaissance England*; and E. M. W. Tillyard, *The Elizabethan World Picture: A Study of the Idea of Order in the Age of Shakespeare, Donne, and Milton*.

8. See, for example, Lawrence Venuti, *Our Halcyon Dayes: English Prerevolutionary Texts and Post-Modern Culture*; Harry R. Garvin, ed., *Romanticism, Modernism, Postmodernism*; and Michael McCanles, *Dialectical Criticism and Renaissance Literature*.

9. Richard Ellmann, *Oscar Wilde*, 430–31, footnote.

10. The idea of Wilde as a post-Modernist is, of course, not new but continually being rediscovered. See, for example, Dollimore, "Different Desires," 36ff., but even that label strikes me as restrictive when applied to his work.

11. Christopher Nassaar, *Into the Demon Universe*, 136–40.

JOHN PAUL RIQUELME

Oscar Wilde's Aesthetic Gothic: Walter Pater, Dark Enlightenment, and The Picture Of Dorian Gray

"J'ai soif de ta beauté."

—Oscar Wilde, *Salomé*[1]

It was from within, apparently, that the foulness and horror had come.
—Oscar Wilde, *The Picture of Dorian Gray*

Gothic Chiaroscuro and Realism

The Picture of Dorian Gray proceeds against the background of Walter Pater's aesthetic writings, but also against Pater in a stronger sense.[2] It provides in narrative form a dark, revealing double for Pater's aestheticism that emerges from a potential for dark doubling and reversal within aestheticism itself. The duplication produces not a repetition of Pater but a new version of his views that says what he cannot or will not articulate, including a recognition of the dark dynamics of doubling and reversal that inhabit those views. That recognition includes the possibility that the process of doubling and reversal will continue. In the novel, Wilde responds to Pater by projecting the dark implications of Pater's attitudes and formulations in a mythic Gothic narrative of destruction and self-destruction. Wilde simultaneously aestheticizes the Gothic and gothicizes the aesthetic. The merger is possible, and inevitable, because of the tendency of Gothic writing to present a fantastic world of indulgence and boundary-crossing and the tendency of the

From *Modern Fiction Studies* 46, no. 3 (Fall 2000): 609–31. Copyright © 2000 by the Purdue Research Foundation by the Johns Hopkins University Press.

aesthetic, in Pater, to press beyond conventional boundaries and to recognize terror within beauty. As an avatar of Narcissus, Dorian Gray embodies both tendencies in a poisonous, self-negating confluence signifying madness. But the madness is not his alone. He shares it with others in the narrative and with the fantastic quality of his story. No one is immune from the madness and its effects. In this allegory about art, Wilde's book and its producer are themselves implicated. They cannot stand apart in a realm of clarity that is somehow insulated from the darkness they portray and embody. Despite the mannered elegance of the book's characters and its style, it sheds only partial light on its subject, which includes itself.

The novel's narrative concerns a dark and darkening recognition that transforms Dorian's life by actualizing a potential that was already there in his family, a potential that is one truth about British society.[3] This dark enlightenment is rendered in a narrative that provides the equivalent of chiaroscuro, understood with reference to painting as a combination of light and clarity with enigmatic darkness and obscurity in a space that undermines the coherence and implied sanity of a representational geometry. By combining clarity and obscurity, often in a shallowly rendered space, chiaroscuro provides an alternative and a challenge to visual representations that rely on general illumination, the appearance of a coherent Cartesian geometry, and a vanishing point. The impression can be enigmatic or frightening for the person whose vision is impeded, because terror tends to arise when insufficient or uneven light creates a sense of disorientation and confusion. Edmund Burke makes this point in his treatise on the sublime and the beautiful.[4] Things that go bump in the night scare us, especially if we cannot see them clearly and understand them by means of familiar categories.

The alternative and the challenge to realism in Wilde's literary chiaroscuro concern realism's reliance on positive knowledge and on believable representations that create for the reader an impression of sanity, intelligibility, and control. The narrative provides in the painting and the book a look at the dark as well as the light, at something disturbing that exceeds, as Gothic writing regularly does, the boundaries of realistic representation and the limits of bourgeois values. As a Gothic revisionary interpretation of Pater's late Romanticism, this particular instance of excess marks a turning point in literary history toward literary modernism. The reliance on doubling as a symptom of a darkness within both culture and the mind follows Robert Louis Stevenson's *The Strange Case of Dr Jekyll and Mr Hyde* (1886) and anticipates Bram Stoker's *Dracula* (1897) and Joseph Conrad's writings, especially *Heart of Darkness* (1902) and *The Secret Sharer* (1910). The conjoining of light and dark occurs as the narrative of a doubling that becomes visible through acts of aesthetic making and aesthetic response. The collaborative act of creating the painting brings into being something apparently new, original, and masterful that turns out to be not only beautiful but also atavistic and terrifyingly at odds with the public values of the society that applauds its beautiful appearance. That collaborative act parallels and engages with our own act of reading. It comes to an end at the same time as our engagement with the book reaches closure, once Dorian and his painting are finished.

Pater Against Wilde: Poe, the French Connection, and Doubling

In *Oscar Wilde*, an award-winning biography, Richard Ellmann claims that in his review of *The Picture of Dorian Gray*, Pater objects only to the portrayal of "Lord Henry Wotton, who speaks so many of Pater's sentences." "But otherwise he was delighted with the book" (323). This is one of Ellmann's least convincing readings, since it is deaf to the irony of Pater's response, which is defensive, prejudicial, and patronizing. Like many other critics, Ellmann reads Pater's review as positive.[5] In fact, Wilde and Pater had exchanged compliments about some of their earlier writings. Pater wrote admiringly to Wilde about *The Happy Prince* in June 1888 (Wilde, *Letters* 219). And Wilde's anonymous review of Pater's *Imaginary Portraits* a year earlier refers to the prose as "wonderful," though he comments that it is ascetic and in danger of becoming "somewhat laborious" (qtd. in Ellmann 289). But in his later review of Pater's *Appreciations* in March 1890, Wilde's criticisms are blunter and more frequent. He says that "Style," though the "most interesting" of the essays, is also "the least successful, because the subject is too abstract" (*Artist* 230); that Charles Lamb "perhaps [. . .] himself would have had some difficulty in recognising the portrait given of him"; that the essay on Samuel Taylor Coleridge "is in style and substance a very blameless work" (232); and that the essay on William Wordsworth "requires re-reading" (234), though he does not say why. Most damning are his comments on Pater's style: "Occasionally one may be inclined to think that there is, here and there, a sentence which is somewhat long, and possibly, if one may venture to say so, a little heavy and cumbersome in movement" (231). Wilde ends with apparently high praise by saying that Pater's work is "inimitable," but also that "he has escaped disciples" (234), presumably including Wilde himself.

Critics who emphasize the positive character of Walter Pater's review of the novel may do so primarily because many of the other reviews were more pointedly negative, even censoriously so.[6] Only by contrast with the hostile reviews can Pater's be called favorable. On the one hand, Pater was generously siding with Wilde against his troglodytic detractors. But considering Wilde's review of *Appreciations* and his echoing of Pater's views in the words of Lord

Henry Wotton, Pater had reasons to be displeased and to pay Wilde back. Ellmann does trace Wilde's shift from an enthusiastic, admiring response to Pater's writings and to aestheticism at Oxford toward his later, more critical stance, but he does not suggest that Pater would have sensed the rift and responded in kind.[7] The details of the review indicate that he did.

In his review, Pater writes as though he were immune from the book's implications, or as though he wishes he were. Taking into account Lord Henry's repetition of Pater's language, which Ellmann mentions without detailing, it becomes clear that Pater could not have missed the novel's challenge to his own attitudes. Unlike Lamb, he recognized his own portrait. Pater attempts to turn aside the book's force in various ways. Like Lord Henry Wotton and Basil Hallward in their responses to Dorian and his portrait, Pater does not want to admit the bearing that Wilde's Gothic rendering has on his own ideals. He takes exception to Wilde's portrayal of an aesthetic hedonism but not by strategies that effectively answer the challenge, for Wilde's resistance approaches the absolute in its ironic probing of Paterian views and the British society into which they fit all too comfortably. Wilde anticipates Pater's response to seeing his own portrait in *Picture*. In chapter 13, Dorian murders the artist who has painted him, in effect murdering the man who, like a father or mentor, has contributed in a significant way to making him what he is. Just before he dies, Basil Hallward sees the painting late at night by the light of a "half-burned candle" (314) in the former schoolroom of Dorian's house, in a scene that would require for visual rendering a candlelit chiaroscuro like that of paintings by Georges de La Tour (1593–1652). By the "dim light," Hallward sees "a hideous face on the canvas grinning at him" that combines "horror" with "marvellous beauty" in a portrayal of its subject that includes "his own brush-work" and a frame of "his own design" (314–15). When he holds the lighted candle to the picture, he finds "his own name" as signature. Hallward's response anticipates Pater's review of the book, for the painter sees at first only "some foul parody" that he feels cannot be his work: "He had never done that. Still, it was his own picture" (315). As subjective and objective genitive, the phrase "his own picture" suggests both that the painting is one he has produced and that it portrays him.

Like Hallward in the schoolroom, Pater finds in Wilde's *Picture* "a satiric sketch," especially with regard to Lord Henry, in which the presentation of "Epicurean theory" "fails" because it abandons "the moral sense." While Pater finds Dorian "a beautiful creation," he calls him "a quite unsuccessful experiment in Epicureanism, in life as a fine art" ("Novel" 265). In his closing statement, having already mentioned the "Doppelgänger," or "double life," as central to Wilde's narrative, Pater is right to associate Wilde's work "with that of Edgar Poe, and with some good French work of the same kind, done, probably, in more or less conscious imitation of it" (266). His assertion implies that *Picture* is also an act of imitation, but of American and French sources, not a British original. Wilde, in fact, does not *imitate* a British writer; he *echoes* his writing. He does so for the same reason that the mythological figure Echo repeats already existing language: in order to say something quite different. Pater would rather not admit that his own writings are at least as important as Poe's in the texture of Wilde's novel and that they are the object of the satire. He also faces only indirectly how thoroughly Wilde's transformation of aesthetic theory is fused with anti-British attitudes. Pater makes the non-British character of the book and its author clear at the start and the end of the review. Besides closing by drawing attention to foreign models rather than one that is much closer to home, Pater begins with comments that situate Wilde prejudicially as an Irish writer. The book putatively produced on non-British patterns by an Irish writer is, not surprisingly, filled with anti-British sentiments. Wilde has turned the critical direction of the Gothic inward, toward England and toward art as an English writer presents it.

At the start of the review, by means of irony and implication, Pater comes close to responding directly in kind to the book's national antagonism, closer than he ever comes to articulating openly his individual antagonism about the transforming of his own work. He may well have sensed that Wilde's skepticism about the British and about Pater's aestheticism were not separable. Misrepresenting or misunderstanding Wilde's emphatic differences from Matthew Arnold, which are as strong as his differences from Pater's aestheticism, Pater suggests that Wilde "carries on, more perhaps than any other writer, the brilliant critical work of Matthew Arnold" ("Novel" 263). Because Pater's own critical directions include significant disagreements with Arnold, by aligning Wilde with Arnold, he distances the younger writer from himself. He would have been intent on doing that in order to separate his own version of aestheticism from the dark version Wilde attributes to him by implication in the novel. Pater describes the ostensible carrying forward of Arnold as "startling" Wilde's "'countrymen.'" By putting "countrymen" in quotation marks, Pater implies ambiguously that, by following in the footsteps of an English critic who had written about the inevitable, necessary "fusion of all the inhabitants of these islands into one homogeneous, English-speaking whole" (Arnold, "On" 296), Wilde surprises his adoptive countrymen, the British, whose countryman he is not, and that he surprises his real countrymen, the Irish, from whom he must have estranged himself by his switching of allegiance.[8] Pater's antagonism toward his younger contemporary is clear in the review's first two sentences. He suggests that Wilde is "an excellent talker," presumably like all the other voluble Irish, whose work relies on the paradox that written dialogue presents itself as spoken. That paradox participates, according to Pater, in a "crudity" that is acceptable only because of what he terms, drawing on another cliché about the Irish, Wilde's "genial, laughter-loving sense of life and its enjoyable intercourse" ("Novel" 263). Under attack, Pater reacts prejudicially to a work by an Irish author who echoes negatively Pater's own writing as part of its presentation of British society's hypocrisy. Although Pater might be willing to admit some of the ills of British society, he cannot do so in a way that implicates himself. Hallward recognizes when he holds "the light up again to the canvas" that "[i]t was from within, apparently, that the foulness and horror had come" (*Picture* 316). Although Wilde's character locates the source of the horror inside, the major British proponent of aestheticism turns away from the implication. Pater also writes about something within emerging to the surface when he describes the Mona Lisa in a passage that Wilde takes as his antithetical model: "It is a beauty wrought out from within upon the flesh [. . .]" (*Renaissance* 80).

When Pater comments on the Doppelgänger in the novel as the experience "not of two *persons*, in this case, but of the man and his portrait" ("Novel" 266) he points toward but does not describe the novel's complex antirealistic structure of doublings.[9] Rather than presenting the book's alternative to realism in its combination of antirealistic and realistic detail, Pater praises and blames the realistic elements as an "intrusion of real life" that, because it is "managed, of course, cleverly enough," "should make his books popular" (264). Pater damns by faint praise when he suggests that Wilde's writing is cleverly crude enough to attract a crowd. In fact, the combination of realistic and antirealistic elements is a pervasive stylistic sign of the novel's dual quality. The doubling structure of the narrative and the narration implicates the reader of *Picture*, including the reviewer of the book, as the counterpart of the picture's viewer. Instead of bringing out the book's complexity, relying on the hierarchical presuppositions of evolutionary thinking about culture, Pater criticizes Wilde for moving away from a "true Epicureanism" toward something "less complex," and presumably less valuable (264). The narrative's intricate doublings, which derive not only from Poe but from Pater's comments on the Mona Lisa, include a multitude of parallels that anticipate a related complexity in *Dracula*. Because the parallels are so numerous and sometimes involve apparent reversals of position, as is often the case in the modern Gothic, the clear distinction between victim and perpetrator, innocent and guilty, blurs, especially when they change roles. As with the doublings of *Dracula*, the reader is invited to feel implicated.

Central to the novel's structure is the doubling not only of person and painting that Pater mentions but also of picture and book, both the book within the narrative that Lord Henry gives Dorian, and the book we read that is also a *Picture*. The doublings include Basil Hallward and Lord Henry

Wotton as fraternal collaborators in the production of the painting and as doubles of different kinds for Dorian himself. Hallward and Wotton split up the dual role that Leonardo da Vinci fills as the quintessential artist-scientist. As a detached experimenter with human lives, Wotton is an avatar of Victor Frankenstein, who produces an ugly, destructive double of himself. There is, as well, the parallel between Dorian Gray and Sybil Vane, as attractive young people to whom unpleasant, destructive revelations are made. Complicating that parallel is the fact that Dorian stands in relation to Sybil as Lord Henry does to him as the revealer of something harsh and damaging. Dorian also stands eventually in the same relation to Basil, whom he destroys, as he has already destroyed Sybil. At the end, he stands in that same destructive relation to himself. Although Dorian prevents Basil from ripping up the painting with a knife near the end of chapter 2, he ultimately stabs the painter, who says he has revealed himself in the painting, and he pursues Hallward's intention from chapter 2 by trying to stab the painting in the book's final chapter and thereby stabbing its subject. This is ekphrasis with a vengeance and the revenge of the ekphrastic object, which strikes out at the artist and viewer, who wish also to strike it.[10] The roles in revolution become indistinguishable.

So many doublings and shifts of position undermine the possibility of reading the book as realistic, that is, as containing primarily intelligible patterns and answers rather than enigmas that cannot be readily resolved. There is no ultimately controlling perspective based on a geometry of narrative relations that allows us to find a stable, resolving point of vantage. In this narrative garden of forking paths, there appears to be a virus that replicates itself in double, antithetical forms within a maze that leads us not to an exit but to an impasse. The narrative oscillations and echoes arising from and as multiple parallels, reversals, and blurrings are modernist in character, but important details identify the writings of Pater as one of their origins. The brushstrokes and the frame are his. As Wilde says in his "Preface," "[I]t is the spectator, and not life, that art really mirrors" (*Picture* 139). And as he suggests in another epigram, the reader as Caliban who sees his face in the mirror of art is likely to be enraged or, like Dorian, driven mad. These epigrams pertain to Pater as an inevitable early reader of the novel and to us.

Wilde Against Pater: Echo Against Narcissus

As I have already suggested, Wilde neither imitates nor follows Pater in his aesthetic Gothic narrative. Instead, he echoes him as a way to evoke, refuse, and transform what he finds in the earlier writer. This is the work of Echo, whose story is bound up with that of Narcissus. In *Picture*, Wilde provides an early example of what T. S. Eliot called "the mythical method," a defining element of modernism that Eliot locates in James Joyce's *Ulysses* and

earlier in some of William Butler Yeats's poems.[11] In fact, the first examples
of the mythical method antedate considerably the examples that Eliot gives.
As early as Thomas Hardy's *The Mayor of Casterbridge* (1886), we find a long
narrative set in recent times that is constructed around extended mythic and
literary parallels. Wilde also constructs his narrative around a myth, that of
Echo and Narcissus. At first it might seem that Narcissus is the primary
mythic figure in *Picture* and that the resulting narrative is not comparable
in its mythic dimension to either *A Portrait of the Artist as a Young Man* or
Ulysses, because the myths surrounding Daedalus and Odysseus are more
various and extended than that of Narcissus. But, in fact, Echo and Narcissus, however different from each other, are counterparts, whose stories
constitute a single compound myth. Echo as well as Narcissus plays a continuing role in Wilde's novel because of the style's echoic character. By echoing Pater's writings frequently and strategically, Wilde projects the story of a
contemporary Narcissus as one truth about Paterian aestheticism. He echoes
Pater not in order to agree with the older British writer's views but to present
them darkly, in shades of gray, as at base contradictory in destructive and
self-destructive ways.

Wilde begins his novel by evoking Pater's aestheticism through a series
of statements about beauty and through allusions to the best-known passages
of Pater's writing: the "Conclusion" of *Studies in the History of the Renaissance*
(1873)[12] and the description of Mona Lisa from the essay on Leonardo da
Vinci in that volume. The first epigram in the "Preface," which asserts that
"[t]he artist is the creator of beautiful things" (*Picture* 138), is followed in the
remaining epigrams by numerous references to "beauty," "beautiful things,"
and "beautiful meanings." As the reader soon discovers, the narrative is permeated by the aesthetic, since it concerns throughout the desire to create,
experience, possess or destroy beauty. Almost immediately, in the second
paragraph of chapter 1, we learn that Lord Henry Wotton sees, along with
"the fantastic shadows of birds in flight," laburnum blossoms "whose tremu-
lous branches seemed hardly able to bear the burden of a beauty so flame-like
as theirs" (140). On the one hand, the branches are personified as undergoing
an ecstatic experience in which they can hardly endure the deep impression
that the blossoms, which they have yielded, or borne, make on them. But their
experience is not unalloyed, for it is also the bearing, or carrying, not of a joy
but of a heavy, awkward "burden" that can hardly be sustained. Further, the
experience includes the play of light and dark in the "fantastic shadows" of
something "in flight," either merely flying or trying to escape.

The passage is of particular note because it contains the first instances
of personification (branches that feel; bees "shouldering their way" through
grass) in a narrative that includes centrally the terrifying coming-to-life

of something inanimate. The crossing of the boundaries between human, animal, and insect in the rhetorical figures of the book's second paragraph anticipates what eventually becomes a matter of animation involving creating and destroying life and a matter of the limits defining the human and civilization. Wilde has merged the aesthetic with issues that regularly arise in Gothic writing, issues that are anthropological, aesthetic, and scientific: the creation of the new and the character of the human. Later in chapter 1, when Hallward tells his friend Lord Henry Wotton about his first encounter with Dorian Gray, he indicates his agreement with something Wotton had told him about the difference between "savages" and "being civilized." The distinction is superficial, since everything depends on appearances: "With an evening coat and a white tie, as you told me once, anybody, even a stock-broker, can gain a reputation for being civilized" (145). Harry had gone out for the evening in public to help prove that "poor artists [...] are not savages." They may not be, but in Basil's case, which asks to be taken as representative, the artist contributes to an ostensibly civilized process of creating art that turns out to unleash a destructive, self-destructive savagery antithetical to the principles of civilization itself. In a typically modern transformation of Gothic narrative, the threat in Wilde's novel comes from within culture and within British society, not from foreigners who can be treated as savages. As an Irish writer, Wilde would have been particularly aware of the distinctions the British tended to draw between themselves and ostensibly less civilized racial and national groups who might in some way pose a crude threat, Caliban-like, to British aspirations and identity.

The passage about laburnum is also notable because it initiates three kinds of echoing within the style of the novel. One occurs as language that literally echoes: "blossoms [...] laburnum [...] branches [...] bear [...] burden [...] beauty [...] birds" and "flame-like [...] fantastic [...] flight flitted" (140). The echoic quality of the prose finds one origin in the stories of Poe, the most echoic stylist among earlier prominent figures in the Gothic tradition. In "The Fall of the House of Usher," for example, the opening sentence begins "*D*uring the whole of a *d*ull, *d*ark, and soundless *day* [...] (95). And the title of the story, "*Wil*ʰ*iam Wil*son," about a man with a double, which provides one precursor for *Picture*, includes an echoic doubling. The second form of echo involves repetition of the passage's language or similar language later in the book. Burdens, flames, and shadows occur regularly, often in passages that are significant and significantly related. The phrase "fantastic shadows," with its evocation of the visual impression of chiaroscuro, returns in a way that punctuates at times the stages in Dorian's destructive attempt to hide and to experience who he is. In the opening of chapter 13, when Dorian and Hallward mount the stairs toward the schoolroom in which

Dorian will murder the artist, the "lamp cast fantastic shadows" (313). Later, when Dorian visits opium dens in an attempt to forget, he sees mostly dark windows, "but now and then fantastic shadows were silhouetted against some lamp–lit blind": "They moved like monstrous marionettes, and made gestures like live things" (348–49). These shadows are cast neither by birds nor marionettes but by human beings. The implications of personification have been reversed from the book's opening, since now the human is marked by the loss of consciousness that is memory in Dorian's will to forget and by a monstrous loss of agency.

The word "burden" also occurs at important moments, sometimes in combination with the word "shadow," which becomes associated with the painting as Dorian's double. In chapter 2, when Dorian first looks carefully at the completed painting and appears "with cheeks flushed," "as if he had recognized himself for the first time," he is described as "gazing at the shadow of his own loveliness" (167). The portrait is a kind of mirror that contains not his image with inflamed cheeks but a dark version, a shadow. In chapter 7, Lord Henry sees something similar in Sybil when a "faint blush, like the shadow of a rose in a mirror of silver, came to her cheeks" (231). Toward the end of chapter 8, Dorian thinks that the "portrait was to bear the burden of his shame" (258). After having "lost control" "almost entirely" (282) in chapter 9, Dorian oscillates in a darkly narcissistic way between looking at the portrait with "loathing" and gazing "with secret pleasure, at the misshapen shadow that had to bear the burden that should have been his own" (298).

"Burden" also reappears at very nearly the novel's end, when Dorian castigates Lord Henry for being willing to "sacrifice anybody [. . .] for the sake of an epigram" (370). When Lord Henry responds that "[t]he world goes to the altar of its own accord," his language suggests most obviously a sacrificial altar, but considering Dorian's immediate confession that he has forgotten how to love and wishes he could recover his passion, the word "altar" resonates with the notion of marriage in addition to and together with that of the pain of a sacrifice. In his brief confession, Dorian says that his "own personality has become a burden" and admits his own narcissism: "I am too much concentrated on myself" (370). Lord Henry's similar preoccupation with himself results, as we learn in the next chapter, in his "divorce-case" (377), because his wife has left him for another man. When Dorian meets Victoria, Lord Henry's wife, early in the novel, Lord Henry makes cynical fun of marriage and women as he commands Dorian: "Never marry at all." Dorian readily agrees because he is "putting into practice" "one of your aphorisms," "as I do everything that you say" (191). That latter statement means both that he puts all of Lord Henry's aphorisms into practice and that he obeys Lord Henry's commands, like a slave. The phrasing echoes the marriage ceremony's vow,

"I do," but not to signify the union of partners in a marriage. Shortly before this exchange, Victoria Wotton has commented that Dorian has just repeated "'one of Harry's views'" and that she always hears "'Harry's views from his friends'" (190). The details of these various scenes involving marriage and self-concern bear on the relation of Wilde's narrative to the story of Echo and Narcissus and to the Gothic tradition.

Gothic narratives regularly include attitudes and situations that challenge the institution of marriage. In this regard, they provide a dark reflection of the concern with domesticity in the history of the realistic novel. Wilde's Gothic narrative is no exception in its presentation of attitudes that make meaningful marriage impossible. Among Wilde's modern innovations is the fusing of a Gothic emphasis on impediments to marriage with the myth of Narcissus, which includes centrally the refusal of Echo's advances. Narcissus would rather not be distracted from gazing at himself. Wilde merges aesthetic narcissism with the Gothic tradition's representation of marriage's difficulty or even impossibility. Further, Victoria Wotton's comment about Dorian's parroting of Lord Henry's views reveals Dorian to be an empty echo, one without a mind of its own. Instead of repeating in order to transform or even counter meaningfully someone else's words, Dorian is the slave of another's attitudes. Echo as a mythological figure represents the possibility of choice under difficult circumstances. Dorian's behavior and his thinking are, by contrast, chosen for him, just as he chooses and manipulates the actions and thoughts of others.

The third type of echo initiated by the laburnum passage is the repeating of words from Pater's aesthetic writings. Throughout his career, Wilde had a reputation for using other writers' language in ways that drew comments amounting to the charge of plagiarism.[13] In that respect, his writing anticipates Eliot's later sometimes unacknowledged borrowings, which challenge Romantic views of the artist's originality. In the case of both writers, their modernist, anti-Romantic borrowings are intentional, motivated, and, because of the new implications of the repeated language, creative. In the laburnum passage, the compound "flame-like" in association with la*burn*um and with birds who are escaping or departing creates a clear echoic link to the "Conclusion" of *The Renaissance*. There Pater closes his first paragraph with the oddly phrased, memorable statement that "[t]his at least of flame-like our life has, that it is but the concurrence, renewed from moment to moment of forces parting sooner or later on their ways" (150). Fire, so prominent in Pater's "Conclusion" in both "flame-like" and "to burn always with this hard, gem-like flame" (152), appears in Dorian's retrospective insight about his boyhood: "Life suddenly became fiery-coloured to him. It seemed to him that he had been walking in fire. Why had he not known it?" (*Picture* 160). Later, Lord

Henry thinks in an apparently positive way about "his friend's young fiery-coloured life" (206). But Dorian's flame-like experiences as a child and later are painful or even infernal, not ecstatic in the way that Pater's "Conclusion" suggests. Wilde's references to flame evoke Pater, but the implications have been reversed. In *Picture*, it is not the flame of art and passion that we choose as our future. Instead, flames of an unpleasant kind have already made us what we are. The flame and its passionate intensity are destructive in Wilde, rather than being the salvation from destruction or a consolation for it.

Dorian's fiery experience also connects him to Narcissus. Lord Henry has already identified Dorian with Narcissus in chapter 1, when he contrasts Basil with Dorian and intellect with beauty: "'Why my dear Basil, he is a Narcissus, and you—well, of course you have an intellectual expression, and all that. But beauty, real beauty, ends where an intellectual expression begins. Intellect is in itself a mode of exaggeration, and destroys the harmony of any face'" (142). Like separating creativity from criticism, which Wilde addresses in "The Critic as Artist" (*Artist* 340–408), severing the tie between beauty and thinking is a mistake that Wilde does not let stand. In Ovid, Narcissus is *inflamed* by his own beauty, which leads him to self-destruction.[14] In Wilde, as later in part III of Eliot's *The Waste Land*, the modern Narcissus is grotesque: a young man with a physically and morally ugly double in Wilde; a young man with an inflamed, carbuncular face who inhabits an infernal contemporary city in Eliot. When Wilde's Narcissus looks into the mirror of his painting, coproduced by his older friends, Basil and Henry, he becomes fascinated first with his own beauty but then with a growing ugliness that he recognizes as also himself.

Mona Lisa as Dark Narcissus/Narcissus as Medusa

The details of Wilde's narration imply that the intense experience central to Paterian aestheticism evoked in the "Conclusion" of *The Renaissance* is narcissistic in character. Wilde established the connection to Pater primarily, as Ellmann points out, by having Lord Henry speak "many of Pater's sentences," or, at least, many sentences that echo Pater. But Lord Henry speaks many of Wilde's sentences as well, and some of those Wildean sentences mimic Pater in their phrasing. Since at Oxford Wilde "adopted 'flamelike' as one of his favorite adjectives" (Ellmann 48), the sentence about the laburnum echoes ambiguously both Pater and Wilde. Although we may be inclined to judge Lord Henry more harshly than the novelist because of his evident misogyny and his general moral blindness, Lord Henry's wit is often in the mode of Oscar Wilde. There is a critical portrait of the artist in progress, as well as a critical portrayal of someone else. In one of his letters, Wilde himself points to his suffused identification with all the major characters in the novel: "I am so glad you like that strange coloured book of mine: it contains much of me in it. Basil Hallward is what I think I am: Lord Henry what the world thinks me: Dorian what I would like to be—in other ages, perhaps" (*Letters* 352). Though Wilde holds Pater's views up for inspection, even mockingly, he does not do so in a self-congratulatory, distanced, or morally superior way. By blurring the distinction between the observer and the subject being observed, Wilde participates in the book's logic of doubling and reversal. If he did not, he would risk adopting a morally superior stance that occupies a position outside the process he presents. The dynamics of his literary chiaroscuro prevent his becoming merely a spectator of the sort that Lord Henry seems to think he is. The critical observer's uncertainty extends to the observer's perspective. Otherwise, that perspective can be narcissistic and blind to its own tendencies, in the way that Lord Henry's self-delusion is, even late in the novel. In the penultimate chapter, despite abundant evidence of Dorian's crimes, Lord Henry refuses to see his dark side, calling him "the young Apollo" (383).

Wilde constructs his narrative around an experience that resembles not only the one Narcissus undergoes but the one that Pater mentions in the final paragraph of the "Conclusion" (153) when he turns to the "awakening" in Jean Jacques Rousseau of "the literary sense" that is described in Rousseau's *Confessions*. Pater devotes part of the paragraph to relating how fear of death inspired Rousseau to "make as much as possible of the interval that remained." He concludes that "our one chance lies in expanding the interval, in getting as many pulsations as possible into the given time." Wilde models Dorian Gray's recognition, as he is sitting for his portrait, and the direction that his life takes on Pater's rendition of Rousseau's life story, but Wilde's version is unremittingly dark by comparison with Pater's. Even the name "Dorian Gray" captures the darkening of what should be a bright beauty, since "Dorian" obviously suggests a Greek form, while "Gray" as a color stands in contrast to Apollonian brightness. In writing about the Renaissance, which involves centrally a revival of classical art and thinking, Pater aligns himself with a cultural heritage that includes the "Dorian," but not with tones of gray, understood as either neutral or dark. As Linda Dowling argues, because of the work of Karl Otfried Müller as transmitted by Benjamin Jowett at Oxford, in the latter part of the nineteenth century, the surname "Dorian" also carried suggestions of pederasty deriving from Greek culture.[15] "Dorian Gray" is oxymoronic in a Paterian context. "Gray" blunts the force and implications of "Dorian," and it does so without suggesting vividly a fruitful merger of opposites of the sort that we find in Joyce's revisionary evocation and extension of Pater at the conclusion of part four of *A Portrait of the Artist as a Young Man*. In that climactic portion of Joyce's narrative, whose title echoes the title and the tale of Wilde's book as "a portrait of the artist" (*Picture* 144), Stephen Dedalus, who like Dorian has a Greek name, sees a rim of the moon on the horizon as if stuck into the earth in a union of heaven and earth that is compared to a "silver hoop embedded in grey sand" (Joyce 173). The grayness of Dorian's story yields no such positive, generative mergers. Joyce's modernist mergings in *A Portrait* combine elements of a Paterian prose style with a myth about a creator and with realistic writing. Wilde's antecedent mergings in *The Picture* combine similar elements, though the myth concerns self-absorption, with the Gothic in a darkly modernist move away from aestheticism and late Romanticism, a move that echoes Pater but also exorcises him.

The echoing as exorcism proceeds through the combining of the light and the dark from Pater in a narrative of recognition and delusion structured around the myth of Narcissus. Rousseau's awakening through literature brings into the narrative an optimistic element from Pater's "Conclusion" that for Dorian is dark. The book that Harry gives him is poisonous. But the narrative is more the story of a painting than a book, though the book is important, as it is in both of Pater's long narratives, *Marius the Epicurean* (1885) and *Gaston de Latour* (1896).[16] When Lord Henry calls the portrait "the finest portrait of modern times" (166), the comparison to the Mona Lisa is inevitable. The work is a new Mona Lisa. The story of the picture's creation, however, fuses details from Pater's description of the Mona Lisa with Rousseau's moment of recognition that has become the experience of Narcissus recognizing his own beauty. Pater suggests that Mona Lisa's sitting for her portrait was possible only through an accompaniment: "by artificial means, the presence of mimes and flute-players, that subtle expression was protracted on the face" (*Renaissance* 79). As Lord Henry talks to Dorian, Hallward realizes that "a look had come into the lad's face that he had never seen there before" (159). Dorian compares the effect to that of music but realizes that it was created by words (160), as if a literary text were being performed. The recognition that this male version of Mona Lisa experiences is clearly that of Narcissus: "A look of joy came into his eyes, as if he had recognized himself for the first time. [. . .] The sense of his own beauty came on him like a revelation" (167). But the recognition is equally of something dark: "There was a look of fear in his eyes, such as people have when they are suddenly awakened" (162). Although that fear comes from Dorian's recognition of his mortality, for which Rousseau found compensation in words, it comes as well from recognizing something monstrously threatening. When Pater looks at the Mona Lisa, he sees not unalloyed beauty but "the unfathomable smile, always with a touch of something sinister in it, which plays over all Leonardo's work" (*Renaissance* 79). This is a beauty that the Greeks would "be troubled by," a "beauty into which the soul with all its maladies has passed." Finally, this is a beauty inseparable from monstrosity: "like the vampire, she has been dead many times, and learned the secrets of the grave" (80).

Late in the novel, Wilde reiterates the connection to the Mona Lisa as Pater presents the painting. Just after calling Dorian "Apollo," Lord Henry says to him that "it has all been to you no more than the sound of music"; he goes on that "[l]ife is a question of nerves, and fibres and slowly built-up cells" (383). As Pater says of Mona Lisa, her vampiric experience "has been to her but as the sound of lyres and flutes." In the same passage, he claims that "it is a beauty wrought out from within upon the flesh, the deposit, little cell by cell, of strange thoughts and fantastic reveries and exquisite passions" (*Renaissance* 80). The darkness is already there, within the painting, waiting for the sitter, Narcissus-like, to behold, to fear, and to desire. Like Patrick Bateman, who videotapes some of his crimes in *American Psycho*, Dorian imagines that "there would be real pleasure in watching it" (259). Later, we hear more about Dorian's desires in passages that echo Pater on the Mona Lisa but with reversed valences. The vocabulary of "cell" and "thought" is still there, but ugliness has displaced beauty. We learn that a single "thought" "crept" from "cell to cell of his brain": "Ugliness that had once been hateful to him because it made things real, became dear to him now for that very reason. Ugliness was the one reality" (349). But Dorian is wrong. There are always two realities, and they are perpetually turning into each other.

The novel is replete with evocations of Narcissus, from Lord Henry's early statement to Basil (142) to Dorian's gazing in the final chapter into the "curiously carved mirror" (387), given to him by Lord Henry, just before he breaks it. In that last chapter, however, the mythic references undergo a metamorphosis when Dorian thinks of the mirror as a "polished shield" immediately prior to discarding it. He has earlier thought of the picture itself as a mirror or has compared himself in a mirror to his deformed image in the undead portrait. At the end of chapter 8, it is "the most magical of mirrors" (259) for observing secrets. Two chapters later, the double image of his laughing face in the mirror and "the evil and aging face" of the portrait pleases him: "The very sharpness of the contrast used to quicken his sense of pleasure" (282). In the ultimate chapter, Dorian is not pleased with the mirror or the painting. The myth of Echo and Narcissus has now merged with that of Medusa and Perseus, whose protection includes a polished shield. Dorian as Narcissus-become-Perseus is about to look at himself-as-Medusa without benefit of his shield and with a knife rather than a sword in hand. The introduction of Medusa here again takes up a prominent detail from Pater's writing and puts it to new use. In the Leonardo essay, Pater devotes an entire vivid paragraph to Leonardo's painting of *Medusa* rendered "as the head of a corpse" (*Renaissance* 68). The paragraph culminates the part of the essay in which Pater evokes the "interfusion of the extremes of beauty and terror" in "grotesques" (67). He says of the painting that "the fascination of corruption penetrates in every touch its exquisitely finished beauty" (68). In *Marius the Epicurean*, Pater uses the image again prominently three times. In the last, most memorable instance, in the closing of chapter 21, he merges Medusa implicitly with Narcissus: "Might this new vision, like the malignant beauty of pagan Medusa, be exclusive of any admiring gaze upon anything but itself?" (*Marius* 202).

Dorian is about to experience the effect of Medusa, which is himself, but, in fact, he has already had this experience. The morning after he murders Basil, while he waits impatiently for Alan Campbell to arrive, Dorian turns his eyes inward, where his "imagination, made grotesque by terror" has become merely a "puppet," the inanimate but dancing image of a person. Time dies and drags "a hideous future from its grave," which it shows to him: "He stared at it. Its very horror made him stone" (327). Like Pater's vampiric Mona Lisa, he has "learned the secrets of the grave" (*Renaissance* 80). Like Medusa, the terrifyingly attractive recognition of his mortality turns him to stone; it dehumanizes him by robbing him of his ordinary human passion. Long before the book's final chapter, Dorian has become undead, still living but not alive as a human being. When Dorian looks at the painting a final time after breaking the mirror, he understands that the Medusa-like truth about the painting is the truth about him. The enraged self-destruction that follows is the demise of Medusa were she able to look at her own poisonous self or, Perseus-like, to use a sharp weapon against herself. On the one hand, the ending restores order and sanity to the narrative by apparently re-establishing the difference between art and life, between the inanimate and the living, between the beautiful and the ugly. But within the seemingly restored realism, a myth darker than the story of Narcissus that involves a mirror has fused with the tale of Narcissus and taken up residence within the ostensible realism, from which it cannot be separated.

If the vampire can live within Mona Lisa, the death of Dorian Gray can be the death of Medusa. In addition to this odd ultimate brushstroke in the novel's mythic surface, which resists explanation, other details of the ending remain enigmatic. We still do not know where we stand in relation to the darkness and the light. There is no vanishing point and no orienting perspective. The beautiful creature became a destroyer who eventually destroyed himself. But how are we to understand and name the avenger's act of revenge against himself, a dark Narcissus's divorce from himself, a suicidal Medusa's look at herself that is also a suicidal Perseus's gazing at Medusa without a shield: as a fit of madness? as a mistake? as an action consciously intended? All we know is that art and life, the beautiful and the ugly, the light and the dark, those counterparts whose relations have been unstable throughout the narrative, have changed places once again. For readers, there is no more consolation, resolution, or explanation in the ending than Basil Hallward experiences when he gazes at "his own picture" and realizes that "It was from within, apparently, that the foulness and the horror had come" (316).

NOTES

1. "I am thirsty for thy beauty" (80; my translation). Salomé speaks these words to the severed head of John the Baptist near the end of the play just before Herod orders her to be killed. I cite from the French version of the play, originally published in Paris in 1893, as the only published version indisputably of Wilde's sole authorship. In *The Writings of Oscar Wilde*, Isobel Murray describes briefly the publication history of the play in her statement concerning the text that accompanies her reprinting of the English translation published in Wilde's lifetime (614).

2. Many critics who write about Wilde or Pater touch on the relation their works bear to each other. Critics who deal at some length with Wilde and Pater include Julia Prewitt Brown, Denis Donoghue, Richard Ellmann, and Christopher S. Nassaar. Nassaar maintains that Pater's "*The Renaissance* casts a long, sinister shadow across *Picture*, and the entire novel seems to be structured with Pater's book as its focal point" (39). The conclusion that Nassaar draws, however, that Wilde saw art's exploration of evil as somehow separable from life needs more defense than he provides. Brown and Donoghue focus on Wilde's significant swerves from Pater concerning art (Brown) or on the less-than-amicable turn in their relations (Donoghue). Brown cites *Oscar Wilde's Oxford Notebooks* (14–17) as providing "a succinct summary of the major differences between Wilde and Pater" (115n4). In the preface to her study of Wilde, Brown gives the following overview: "Walter Pater's place in the particular intellectual history already alluded to here is relatively minor, and [. . .] far less is said in the following pages about Pater's influence on Wilde than about Wilde's divergence from Pater. With attention to the philosophical significance of Wilde's career, this loosening of the long-established tie between Pater and Wilde constitutes the main revisionary thrust of this book" (xvii). See also Brown 3–4, 49, 59–60. In his main discussion of Wilde's relations with Pater in his biography of Pater, Donoghue maintains that "Pater never really liked Wilde" (81) and that "[t]he friendship [. . .] virtually came to an end in the winter of 1891" (83). I find the argument for significant, defining differences between Wilde and Pater convincing. I pursue some of the differences as they emerge in specific texts in the present essay and in my essay on *Salomé*.

3. Lord Henry investigates Dorian's family background in chapter 3 (175–77), where we learn that it includes passion and violence, as well as class antagonism and a disregard of conventional behavior. Dorian's mother married a subaltern without financial resources, obviously against her father's will. As a consequence, her father, Lord Kelso, arranged to have the subaltern killed in a duel. Dorian's decision to store the portrait in the room set up for him by his grandfather to keep him out of the way after his mother's death suggests that the portrait's meaning emerges in part from the family's history.

4. In section 3 of *A Philosophical Inquiry*, "Obscurity," Burke states: "To make any thing very terrible, obscurity seems in general to be necessary. When we know the full extent of any danger, when we can accustom our eyes to it, a great deal of the apprehension vanishes. Every one will be sensible of this, who considers how greatly night adds to our dread [. . .]" (54).

5. In the midst of reprinting Wilde's letters to editors responding to the antagonistic reviews of his novel, Rupert Hart-Davis includes a footnote that quotes the opening sentence of Pater's review as an example of "some of the most welcome praise," which "came later" (Wilde, *Letters* 270n1). Donald H. Eriksen refers to "Walter Pater's favorable review in the *Bookman*" (99). By contrast, Donoghue sees the praise in later portions of the review as Pater's being "generous" (85) after he had taken "the occasion to repudiate not only Lord Henry but his creator" (84).

6. Rupert Hart-Davis identifies and describes some of the negative reviews when he publishes Wilde's lengthy letters to the editors of the journals in *Letters* (257–72).

7. Ellmann points out that Wilde sent Pater a presentation copy of *Salomé* when it was published in French (374). But Denis Donoghue mentions that "[t]here is no evidence that Pater acknowledged the gift" (85).

8. Arnold expresses these sentiments in "On the Study of Celtic Literature" (291–386). In his use of the word "countrymen," Pater may well have been echoing Arnold's use of that word ("my own countrymen"; "Introduction" 391) to refer unambiguously to the English in his introduction to his study of Celtic literature (387–95).

9. See Chris Baldick's *In Frankenstein's Shadow* for a sketch of some of the book's significant doublings related to the one I provide but emphasizing monstrosity and the multiform character of identity rather than anti-realism and the implicating of the reader (148–152).

10. For studies of the ekphrastic tradition, see Krieger and Hollander.

11. Eliot uses the term in his review of Joyce's *Ulysses*, "Ulysses, Order, and Myth," originally published in *The Dial* (November, 1923).

12. The title of Pater's *Studies* later became *The Renaissance: Studies in Art and Poetry*. As is well known, Pater withdrew his "Conclusion" after the first edition but restored it in revised form for the third edition (1888) and subsequent editions. Donoghue describes the uproar over the "Conclusion" and the steps Pater took in response (48–67).

13. In the introduction to his study of Wilde, Peter Raby describes Wilde's habitual borrowings and the charge leveled against them (9).

14. In Book III of Ovid's *Metamorphoses*, we find: "uror amore mei: flammas moveoque feroque" ("I am inflamed with love for myself: the flames I both fan and bear"; 463) and "sic attenuatus amore / liquitur et tecto paulatim carpitur igni" ("thus ravaged by his love, he melts away, and gradually he is devoured by that buried fire"; 489–90). I am grateful to Melanie Benson of the Boston University Department of English for drawing my attention to the flame imagery in Ovid's presentation of Narcissus and for her translation of the relevant phrases.

15. See especially Dowling 124–125, but also 74 and 79, where she comments on the influence of Müller's *Die Dorier: Geschicten hellnischer Stämme und Städte*.

16. Isobel Murray points out the importance of books to Pater's protagonists in her introduction to Wilde's novel (ix).

Works Cited

Arnold, Matthew. *Lectures and Essays in Criticism. The Complete Prose Works of Matthew Arnold.* Vol. III. Ed. R. H. Super. Ann Arbor: U of Michigan P, 1962.

Baldick, Chris. *In Frankenstein's Shadow: Myth, Monstrosity, and Nineteenth-century Writing.* Oxford: Clarendon, 1987.

Brown, Julia Prewitt. *Cosmopolitan Criticism: Oscar Wilde's Philosophy of Art.* Charlottesville: UP of Virginia, 1997.

Burke, Edmund. *A Philosophical Inquiry into the Origin of Our Ideas of the Sublime and Beautiful.* 1759. Ed. Adam Phillips. Oxford: Oxford UP, 1990.

Conrad, Joseph. *Heart of Darkness.* 1902. New York: Norton, 1978.

———. *The Secret Sharer.* 1910. Ed. Daniel R. Schwarz. Boston: Bedford, 1997.

Donoghue, Denis. *Walter Pater: Lover of Strange Souls.* New York: Knopf, 1995.

Dowling, Linda. *Hellenism and Homosexuality in Victorian Oxford.* Ithaca: Cornell UP, 1994.

Eliot, T. S. "Ulysses, Order, and Myth." *James Joyce: Two Decades of Criticism.* Ed. Seon Givens. New York: Vanguard, 1963. 198–202.

Ellis, Bret Easton. *American Psycho: A Novel.* New York: Vintage, 1991.

Ellmann, Richard. *Oscar Wilde.* New York: Knopf, 1988.

Ericksen, Donald H. *Oscar Wilde.* Boston: Twayne, 1977.

Hardy, Thomas. *The Mayor of Casterbridge.* 1886. Ed. Dale Kramer. New York: Oxford UP, 1987.

Hollander, John. *The Gazer's Spirit: Poems Speaking to Silent Works of Art.* Chicago: U of Chicago P, 1995.

Joyce, James. *"A Portrait of the Artist as a Young Man"; Text, Criticism, and Notes.* Ed. Chester G. Anderson. New York: Viking, 1968.

Krieger, Murray. *Ekphrasis: The Illusion of the Natural Sign.* Baltimore: Johns Hopkins UP, 1992.

Murray, Isobel. "Introduction." *The Picture of Dorian Gray.* Ed. Isobel Murray. Oxford: Oxford UP, 1981. vii–xvi.

Nassaar, Christopher S. *Into the Demon Universe: A Literary Exploration of Oscar Wilde.* New Haven: Yale UP, 1974.

Ovid. *Metamorphoses. Liber 1–5. Ovid's Metamorphoses. Books 1–5.* Ed. William S. Anderson. Norman: U of Oklahoma P, 1997.

Pater, Walter. *Gaston de Latour: an unfinished romance.* Ed. Charles L. Shadwell. London: Macmillan, 1896.

———. *Marius the Epicurean, His Sensations and Ideas.* 1885. Ed. Ian Small. Oxford: Oxford UP, 1986.

———. "A Novel by Mr. Oscar Wilde." *Selected Writings of Walter Pater.* Ed. Harold Bloom. New York: Columbia UP, 1974.

———. *The Renaissance: Studies in Art and Poetry.* 1893. 4th ed. Ed. Adam Phillips. Oxford: Oxford UP, 1986.

Poe, Edgar Allan. *Selected Writings of Edgar Allan Poe.* Ed. Edward H. Davidson. Boston: Houghton Mifflin, 1956.

Raby, Peter. *Oscar Wilde.* Cambridge: Cambridge UP, 1988.

Riquelme, John Paul. "Shalom/Solomon/*Salomé*: Modernism and Wilde's Aesthetic Politics." *The Centennial Review* 39 (1995): 575–610.

Stevenson, Robert Louis. *The Strange Case of Dr Jekyll and Mr Hyde.* 1886. New York: Dell, 1966.

Stoker, Bram. *Dracula.* London: Archibald Constable, 1897.

Wilde, Oscar. *The Artist as Critic: Critical Writings of Oscar Wilde*. 1969. Ed. Richard Ellmann. Chicago: U of Chicago P, 1982.

———. *The Letters of Oscar Wilde*. Ed. Rupert Hart-Davis. New York: Harcourt, 1962.

———. *Oscar Wilde's Oxford Notebooks: A Portrait of a Mind in the Making*. Ed. Philip E.
Smith and Michael S. Helfand. New York: Oxford UP, 1989.

———. *The Picture of Dorian Gray. The Portable Oscar Wilde*. 1946. Ed. Richard Aldington.
New York: Viking, 1965.

———. *Salomé. A Florentine Tragedy. Vera. The First Collected Edition of the Works of Oscar
Wilde*. 1908. Vol. I. Ed. Robert Ross. London: Dawsons of Pall Mall, 1969.

———. *The Writings of Oscar Wilde*. Ed. Isobel Murray. Oxford: Oxford UP, 1989.

CHRISTOPHER S. NASSAAR

Wilde's Salomé and the Victorian Religious Landscape

The chaos of conflicting religious opinions that dominated the Victorian era is distanced, exoticized and reproduced by Wilde in his symbolist one-act play *Salomé*. That some aspects of this play reflect appearances of Victorian life has been recognized by many critics. Salomé has been seen variously as the New Woman (Beckson, Dellamora) and as Decadence personified (Ellmann, Gagnier, Shewan, Dijkstra), while Jokanaan has been interpreted as an embodiment of Victorian celibate Christianity. Bram Dijkstra has written of the general *fin-de-siècle* interest in Salomé that "Salomé's hunger for the Baptist's head thus proved to be a mere pretext for the men's need to find the source of all wrongs they thought were being done to them. Salomé, the evil woman, became their favourite scapegoat." In order for the spirit to triumph over the body, Salomé had to be executed "in a cleansing massacre." Her death became the triumph of the Victorian male over sexual temptation (p. 398). In one of his essays, Richard Ellmann astutely observed that Salomé and Jokanaan embody respectively the Pater and Ruskin strains in Wilde, while Herod reflects Wilde himself, caught between these two opposing influences and unable to decide which one to embrace ("Overtures," pp. 85–90). In the present article, my argument is that all the characters in the play, especially the minor ones, have Victorian counterparts and that the play, as a whole, is meant at one level to dramatize

From *The Wildean* 20 (January 2002): 2–13. Copyright © 2002 by Christopher S. Nassaar.

the entire religious landscape in Victorian England, presenting it to the reader in an exoticized manner.

(i)

In my analysis, I shall begin with the atheists, move on to the adherents of strange religions, then the Jews and Christians, and end with Salomé and her new religion of Decadence. The Cappadocian, for example, is an unmistakable echo of Nietzsche, whose fame had begun to spread throughout Europe by the time Wilde sat down to write his play. *Thus Spake Zarathustra* begins with a famous and central passage:

> Zarathustra went down the mountain alone, no one meeting him. When he entered the forest, however, there suddenly stood before him an old man, who had left his holy cot to seek roots. . . .
> When Zarathustra was alone, however, he said to his heart: "Could it be possible! This old saint in the forest hath not yet heard of it, that *God is dead*!" (pp. 4–6)

The Cappadocian strongly echoes this when he says: "In my country there are no gods left. The Romans have driven them out. There are some who say that they have hidden themselves in the mountains, but I do not believe it. Three nights I have been on the mountains seeking them everywhere. I did not find them. And at last I called them by their names, but they did not come. I think they are dead" (p. 584). Nietzsche's central statement on God is thus distanced, exoticized and injected into *Salomé*.

The chief representative of atheist rationalism in the play, however, is Herodias. When the Jews begin to dispute about their religion, she states impatiently: "Make them be silent. They weary me" (p. 594). A while later, when the Nazarenes start discussing the miracles of Christ, her response is much more vehement: "Ho! Ho! Miracles. I do not believe in miracles. I have seen too many. . . . How these men weary me! They are ridiculous!" (p. 595). Throughout, she dismisses and mocks the prophecies of Jokanaan, insisting on his execution. Atheist rationalism, supported by new scientific discoveries, was a strong intellectual current in Victorian England, and included such prominent figures as Mill, Marx and Hardy. At its most extreme, it not only dismissed religion but mocked and attacked it, as in the case of the Decadents. Pater's atheism and his quiet irritation with Christianity for its supposed suppression of the human spirit is quite apparent in *The Renaissance*, for instance, as when he writes in praise of Winckelmann:

On a sudden the imagination feels itself free. How facile and direct, it seems to say, is this life of the senses and the understanding, when once we have apprehended it! ... How mistaken and round-about have been our efforts to reach it by mystic passion, and monastic reverie; how they have deflowered the flesh; how little they have really emancipated us! (pp. 118)

Aubrey Beardsley mockingly dedicates his highly licentious novel-fragment, *The Story of Venus and Tannhäuser*, to an imaginary cardinal in the Roman Catholic Church. And the minor Decadent poet John Barlas embraces an aesthetic Satanism in his poem *Terrible Love*. Herodias, as a lesser Salomé, is another embodiment of Decadence in the play, and she reflects the extreme anti-religious attitude that was a prominent feature of this movement and which grew out of the current of atheist rationalism in Victorian England.

(ii)

As Christianity weakened during the Victorian period, there was a proliferation of new religions on the scene. Carlyle, for example, lost his Christian faith but propounded a brand of pantheism in *Sartor Resartus* and *The French Revolution*. Arnold reduced God to a power outside ourselves that pushes in the direction of morality but did not eliminate Him altogether from the picture. Yeats and Conan Doyle, among others, became ardent spiritualists. Many post-Darwinists, from Butler to Shaw, adopted the idea of creative evolution in various forms. And Huxley coined the term "agnostic." This chaos of new, often strange religious beliefs is again distanced, exoticized and captured in *Salomé*. The Nubians, for instance, who used to inhabit areas of southern Egypt and northern Sudan, have their own bizarre religion, described by one of them as follows:

The gods of my country are very fond of blood. Twice in the year we sacrifice to them young men and maidens; fifty young men and a hundred maidens. But it seems we never give them quite enough, for they are very harsh to us. (p. 584)

Salomé (who is nominally Jewish but who, like Herod and Herodias, is presented by Wilde as thoroughly pagan) refers to the moon as a goddess who "has never abandoned herself to men, like the other goddesses" (p. 586). The young Syrian is entrapped siren-like by Salomé (the spiritual daughter of the moon-goddess Cybele) and worships her as a kind of deity, ultimately offering himself as a blood sacrifice to her, while the page of Herodias reacts to the princess with knowing terror.

Many of the Caesars of Rome were regarded as part divine, and this is stressed by Wilde through Tigellinus and Herod when they unconsciously use the titles of Christ in describing Caesar:

HEROD: What does that mean? The Saviour of the world.

TIGELLINUS: It is a title that Caesar takes.

HEROD: But Caesar is not coming into Judaea. Only yesterday I received letters from Rome. They contained nothing concerning this matter. And you, Tigellinus, who were at Rome during the winter, you heard nothing concerning this matter, did you?

TIGELLINUS: Sire, I heard nothing concerning the matter. I was explaining the title. It is one of Caesar's titles. . . .

HEROD: Wherefore should I not be happy? Caesar, who is lord of the world, who is lord of all things, loves me well. He has just sent me most precious gifts. Also he has promised me to summon to Rome the King of Cappadocia. who is my enemy. It may be that at Rome he will crucify him, for he is able to do all things that he wishes. Verily, Caesar is lord. (pp. 594–97)

When Salomé emerges from Herod's feast, she escapes not only from his lustful gaze but from an atmosphere of religious debate and confusion which repels her:

SALOMÉ: How sweet the air is here! I can breathe here! Within there are Jews from Jerusalem who are tearing each other in pieces over their foolish ceremonies, and barbarians who drink and drink, and spill their wine on the pavement, and Greeks from Smyrna with painted eyes and painted cheeks, and frizzed hair curled in twisted coils, and silent, subtle Egyptians, with long nails of Jade and russet cloaks, and Romans brutal and coarse, with their uncouth jargon. (p. 586)

The Egyptians, Greeks, barbarians and Romans evoke images of strange religions, for they are associated with the quarrelling Jews and seem quite comfortable in the atmosphere of religious multiplicity and confusion which the Jews create as they argue over the details of Judaism. They are introduced, moreover, against a background of religious disorder. When Herod promises Salomé whatever she may ask for if she will dance for him, he cannot withdraw the oath because "I have sworn by my gods. I know it well" (p. 600). Wilde does not focus on new religions or give them prominence in Salomé, however, for in the Victorian period none of them managed to attract more than a small group of followers: the confrontation remained fundamentally between atheism and Christianity. A second reason is that he himself proposes a new "religion" in this play, and does not want to place it on a level with these other religions; but this will be discussed later on in the essay.

(iii)

Within the Christian faith, the Victorian age was one of great controversy and clashing opinions, and this is reflected in the life of its most prominent religious figure, John Henry Cardinal Newman. Newman never once in his life doubted the existence of God or the basic tenets of Christianity: it was its creeds, doctrines and dogmas that were his main concern. At Oriel College, Oxford, he associated at first with the "Noetics," a fairly liberal group of churchmen who tended to criticize traditional orthodoxies, and whose approach to Christianity was rationalistic. He soon drifted away from them, however, towards friends like Hurrell Froude, Edward Pusey and John Keble, whose religious thought was quite different from the "Noetics" and who questioned the idea that the Anglican Church, as first and ideally conceived, was necessarily Protestant rather than Catholic. With his friends, he established the Oxford Movement, which was anti-rationalistic and anti-liberal in its religious thought and which took the *via media*—the middle way—between the Protestant and Catholic views on tradition and authority. Newman continued to drift towards Catholicism until in 1845 he was received into the Roman Catholic Church. He was a liberal Catholic, however, and was regarded with distrust by his fellow converts and by the Catholic Church in England and Ireland. In 1863–64, he and the Catholic Church were severely attacked by Charles Kingsley, an extreme and popular anti-Catholic divine, and he responded by writing his most famous book *Apologia Pro Vita Sua*, the history of his religious life. The book was warmly received by the English public and Newman became a popular figure once again. In 1878 Protestant Oxford gave him an honorary fellowship. In 1879 the Catholic Church made him a cardinal. He died in 1890, untouched by Darwin's *The Origin of Species* and the entire evolutionary controversy.

This religious conflict within English Victorian Christianity, conveniently mirrored in Cardinal Newman's life, is exoticized and dramatized in the arguing Jews and Nazarenes of Salomé. These must be taken together, for they represent the Judaeo-Christian tradition in a pagan world. It is possible to speculate that Wilde meant them to represent the Protestant and Catholic churches respectively, like the Jews and Jebusites in Dryden's *Absalom and Achitophel*. At any rate, their chief characteristic is religious wrangling. When Herod declares that Jokanaan is a man who has seen God, for instance, the

Jews, who all accept the basic tenets of Judaism, nonetheless manage to come up with five differing opinions:

A JEW: That cannot be. There is no man who has seen God since the prophet Elias. He is the last man who saw God. In these days God does not show Himself. He hideth Himself. Therefore great evils have come upon the land.

ANOTHER JEW: Verily, no man knoweth if Elias the prophet did indeed see God. Peradventure it was but the shadow of God that he saw.

A THIRD JEW: God is at no time hidden. He showeth Himself at all times and in everything. God is in what is evil, even as He is in what is good.

A FOURTH JEW: That must not be said. It is a very dangerous doctrine. It is a doctrine that cometh from the schools at Alexandria, where men teach the philosophy of the Greeks. And the Greeks are Gentiles. They are not even circumcised.

A FIFTH JEW: No one can tell how God worketh. His ways are very mysterious. It may be that the things which we call evil are good, and that the things which we call good are evil. (p. 594)

The Nazarenes, when Christ is mentioned, also display confusion and disagreement, and this is compounded by the Sadducees and Pharisees, two Jewish sects who disagree about the existence of angels, among other things:

FIRST NAZARENE: This Man worketh true miracles. Thus, at a marriage which took place in a little town of Galilee, a town of some importance, He changed water into wine. Certain persons who were present related it to me. Also, He healed two lepers that were seated before the Gate of Capernaum simply by touching them.

SECOND NAZARENE: Nay, it was blind men that He healed at Capernaum.

FIRST NAZARENE: Nay, they were lepers. But He healed blind people also, and He was seen on a mountain talking with angels.

A SADDUCEE: Angels do not exist.

A PHARISEE: Angels exist, but I do not believe that this Man has talked with them.

FIRST NAZARENE: He was seen by a great multitude of people talking with angels.

A SADDUCEE: Not with angels. (p. 595)

Another pillar of Christian morality in Victorian England was John Ruskin, whom Ellmann associates with Jokanaan. Ruskin, whom everyone referred to as a prophet, believed and preached that art and morality are inseparable, indeed that the importance of any work of art should be measured by its moral and spiritual impact on the beholder. The function of art is to create better human beings, to elevate them morally and strengthen them spiritually. Ruskin remained celibate throughout his life, although he did marry a distant cousin, Euphemia Gray, in 1848. After marriage, Ruskin explained to Effie that many early Christians had spent their entire lives in married celibacy, that children would interfere with his work, and that consummation should be delayed for six years or so. He did take her to live in Venice, however, where she displayed a distinct love for dancing and masked balls, and for pleasure and flirtatiousness generally. Although she was never unfaithful to him, Ruskin sometimes felt betrayed by her misconduct. The marriage was annulled in 1854 when Effie fell in love with John Everett Millais, the Pre-Raphaelite painter and Ruskin's friend, whom she subsequently married. Later in life Ruskin fell in love with another young girl, Rose La Touche, and proposed marriage to her in 1866, but her response was that she needed two and possibly four years before she could answer him. He waited in agony but never received an answer; Rose La Touche died young, soon after the end of the fourth year, and Ruskin continued to mourn her death for many years afterwards, as he records in his diary.

It is easy to argue that Jokanaan evokes Ruskin. As Ellmann has observed: "Behind the figure of Jokanaan lurks the image of that perversely untouching, untouchable prophet John whom Wilde knew at Oxford. When Jokanaan, up from his cistern for a moment, cries to Salomé, "Arrière, fille de Sodome! Ne me touchez pas. Il ne faut pas profaner le temple du Seigneur Dieu," a thought of Ruskin, by now sunk down into madness, can scarcely have failed to cross Wilde's mind. . . . Jokanaan is not Ruskin, but he is Ruskinian as Wilde understood that pole of his character" ("Overtures," p. 89). In my view, Jokanaan is not only Ruskinian but is also Wilde's presentation of Christianity as a religion of sexual repression. I have put this idea forward at length in my critical study of Wilde, *Into the Demon Universe* (pp. 94–101), and in subsequent essays, and shall only give a brief recapitulation here. Jokanaan has a hidden lust for Salomé that betrays itself in the language he uses, which often has an unconscious sexual meaning. He refuses to look at her, and voluntarily returns to his symbolic dark underground cistern rather than accept her advances, however, for— Ruskin-like—the idea of sexual contact with her horrifies him. At the same time he is obsessed with her, as with her mother previously, and continually condemns them both. His end—a severed head, eyes closed, sexually consumed by Salomé—really captures his essence, for he possesses the object of his desire but will never be aware of the fact. As Salomé says to the head: "Ah! Wherefore didst thou not look at me, Jokanaan? Behind thy hands and thy curses thou didst hide thy face. Thou didst put upon thine eyes the covering of him who would see his God" (p. 604). Jokanaan uses Christianity as a shield against sexual contact, which he nonetheless unconsciously longs for. As Rodney Shewan has pointed out, Wilde's most famous critic, Richard Strauss, viewed Jokanaan negatively. Shewan has also argued that Jokanaan's "self-esteem is unattractive, almost blasphemous. . . . With his bombast, his priggishness, and his prurient anatomization of Herodias, he can hardly be taken seriously as the voice of the new spiritual kingdom" (p. 136). Through Jokanaan—the chief representative of Christianity in the play—Wilde sought not simply to exoticize Ruskin but also to discredit and dismiss Christianity as a prelude to presenting us with his own "religion." The fall of the Judaeo-Christian tradition, and of Newman and Ruskin, in the play leaves the stage empty for Wilde to fill the void.

(iv)

Salomé, Wilde's main character, embodies the Decadent movement of the Victorian *fin-de-siècle*, but set in a faraway land in biblical times. Wilde associates her with the pagan moon-goddess Cybele, who jealously guarded her virginity, was served by eunuch priests, and murdered her lover, the holy king Attis, after he mated with her (or tried to, depending on the version of the myth). It is Cybele who is the light of the world while Salomé is the incarnation on earth of that light for a brief moment in history. Wilde's play is a kind of Black Mass in which Salomé is presented as a counterpoint to Christ. She is born as the result of a demonic Virgin Birth (Herod insists that his wife is sterile) and brings the world a new gospel of love and complete sexual liberation. Jokanaan's prophecies are often ambiguous and can be read as prophesying the coming of Salomé, with gender confusion, as when he cries out: "So the day is come, the day of the Lord, and I hear upon the mountains the feet of Him who shall be the Saviour of the world" (p. 594). But what does come is Salomé, who dances with naked feet on blood, then both preaches and practises a gospel of total sexual freedom. In Wilde's eyes it is she who is the Saviour of the world, liberating it from the falsities of Christian love. "The mystery of love is greater than the mystery of death. Love only should one consider" (p. 604), she declares chillingly to the grisly blood-soaked head of the dead prophet, thus redefining the word "love" blasphemously in completely sexual terms and insisting on the relentless pursuit of sexual love even at its most perverse. And like Christ, she is murdered at the end for preaching and practising the gospel of love uncompromisingly, but attains immortality in the minds of people—and the hearts of the Decadents.

In *Salomé* Wilde presents us with the entire Victorian religious land-scape exoticized, but is uncompromisingly on the side of the atheists. As a Romantic mythmaker, however, he weaves together a paradoxical aesthetic "religion" of evil and gives it centre-stage in this landscape. In the final analy-sis, Wilde presents himself as the Saviour of the world, offering the Victori-ans an aesthetic Satanism, a mythical "religion" of complete sexual freedom that sanctifies all the various forms of perversion, and accepts the hard core of darkness that he discerned in the depths of the human soul. In *Salomé* Wilde wanted this "religion," and Decadence in general, to stand at the end of the nineteenth century's quest for truth. It is a "religion" that quickly destroyed Wilde, and that Kurtz, a few years later, was to embrace in the jungles of Africa in that post-Decadent masterpiece, *Heart of Darkness*.

WORKS CITED

Beckson, Karl. *London in the 1890s: A Cultural History*. New York: Norton, 1992.

Dellamora, Richard, "Traversing the Feminine in Oscar Wilde's *Salomé*." *In Victorian Sages and Cultural Discourse: Renegotiating Gender in Power*. Ed. Thaïs E. Morgan. New Brunswick, NJ: Rutgers UP, 1990, pp. 246–264.

Cohen, Philip K. *The Moral Vision of Oscar Wilde*. Rutherford, NJ: Fairleigh Dickinson Uni-versity Press, 1978.

Dijkstra, Bram, *Idols of Perversity: Fantasies of Feminine Evil in Fin-de-Siècle Culture*. New York: Oxford University Press, 1986.

Ellmann, Richard. *Oscar Wilde*. New York: Knopf, 1988.

———. "Overtures to *Salomé*." In *Oscar Wilde: Modern Critical Views*. Ed. Harold Bloom. New York: Chelsea House, 1985, pp. 77–90.

Gagnier, Regenia. *Idylls of the Marketplace: Oscar Wilde and the Victorian Public*. Stanford: Stanford UP, 1986.

Hart-Davis, Rupert, ed. *Letters of Oscar Wilde*. New York: Harcourt, Brace and World, 1962.

Nassaar, Christopher S, "Wilde's *The Picture of Dorian Gray* and *Salomé*." *The Explicator* 53:4, 1995, pp. 217–220.

Nassaar, Christopher S. *Into the Demon Universe: A Literary Exploration of Oscar Wilde*. New Haven: Yale University Press, 1974.

Nietzsche, Friedrich. *Thus Spake Zarathustra*. Ed. Oscar Levy. New York: Russell & Russell, 1964.

Pater, Walter. *The Renaissance: Studies in Art and Poetry*. Ed. Adam Phillips. Oxford and New York: Oxford University Press, 1986. An Oxford World's Classics paperback.

Raby, Peter. *Oscar Wilde*. Cambridge: Cambridge University Press, 1988.

Shewan, Rodney. *Oscar Wilde: Art and Egotism*. London: Macmillan, 1977.

Wilde, Oscar. *Complete Works of Oscar Wilde*. Third Edition. Glasgow: HarperCollins, 1994.

BURKHARD NIEDERHOFF

Parody, Paradox and Play in
The Importance of Being Earnest[1]

1. Introduction

*T*he Importance of Being Earnest is an accomplished parody of the conventions of comedy. It also contains numerous examples of Oscar Wilde's most
characteristic stylistic device: the paradox. The present essay deals with the
connection between these two features of the play.[2] In my view, the massive
presence of both parody and paradox in Wilde's masterpiece is not coinci-
dental; they are linked by a number of significant similarities. I will analyse
these similarities and show that, in *The Importance of Being Earnest*, parody
and paradox enter into a connection that is essential to the unique achievement of this play.

2. Parody

The most obvious example of parody in Wilde's play is the anagnorisis
that removes the obstacles standing in the way to wedded bliss for Jack
and Gwendolen. The first of these obstacles is a lack of respectable relatives on Jack's part. As a foundling who was discovered in a handbag at
the cloakroom of Victoria railway station, he does not find favour with
Gwendolen's mother, the formidable Lady Bracknell. She adamantly
refuses to accept a son-in-law "whose origin [is] a Terminus" (3.129).
The second obstacle is Gwendolen's infatuation with the name "Ernest,"
the alias under which Jack has courted her. When she discovers that

From *Connotations* 13, nos. 1–2 (2003/2004): 32–55. Copyright © 2005 by WaxmannVerlag
GmbH.

her lover's real name is Jack, she regards this as an "insuperable barrier" between them (3.51). Both difficulties are removed when the true identity of the foundling is revealed. It turns out that Jack has been christened "Ernest" and that he is Lady Bracknell's nephew. Thus he bears the name that Gwendolen insists on, and he has also acquired respectable relatives—even Lady Bracknell would find it hard to raise convincing objections against herself.

The anagnorisis comes about through a visible sign, a time-honoured method first discussed in Aristotle's *Poetics*. The most famous example of this method, also mentioned by Aristotle,[3] is the scar which Odysseus owes to his courageous fight with a boar and which reveals his identity to his nurse Eurycleia when he returns to Ithaca after an absence of twenty years. In *The Importance of Being Earnest*, the sign that proves Jack's identity is the handbag in which he was found. His former nurse, Miss Prism, explains how the baby ended up in the bag:

Miss Prism. [. . .] On the morning of the day you mention, a day that is for ever branded on my memory, I prepared as usual to take the baby out in its perambulator. I had also with me a somewhat old, but capacious hand-bag in which I had intended to place the manuscript of a work of fiction that I had written during my few unoccupied hours. In a moment of mental abstraction, for which I can never forgive myself, I deposited the manuscript in the bassinette and placed the baby in the hand-bag.

Jack. (*who had been listening attentively*) But where did you deposit the hand-bag?

Miss Prism. Do not ask me, Mr Worthing.

Jack. Miss Prism, this is a matter of no small importance to me. I insist on knowing where you deposited the hand-bag that contained that infant.

Miss Prism. I left it in the cloak-room of one of the larger railway stations in London.

Jack. What railway station?

Miss Prism. (*quite crushed*) Victoria. The Brighton line. (*Sinks into a chair*) [. . .]

Enter Jack with a hand-bag of black leather in his hand

Jack. (*rushing over to Miss Prism*) Is this the hand-bag, Miss Prism? Examine it carefully before you speak The happiness of more than one life depends on your answer.

Miss Prism. (*calmly*) It seems to be mine. Yes, here is the injury it received through the upsetting of a Gower Street omnibus in younger and happier days. Here is the stain on the lining caused by the explosion of a temperance beverage, an incident that occurred at Leamington. And here, on the lock, are my initials. I had forgotten that in an extravagant mood I had had them placed there. The bag is undoubtedly mine. I am delighted to have it so unexpectedly restored to me. It has been a great inconvenience being without it all these years.

(3.344–90)

Even in comedy, anagnorises that bring about family reunions tend to be tearful events, or at least highly emotional ones,[4] but the emphasis placed on Miss Prism's battered old bag undercuts any such sentiments. It introduces the comic incongruity between debased or trivial content and dignified form that figures prominently in most definitions of parody.[5] To Miss Prism, the scene is not about the restoration of a lost child but about the recovery of a handbag. The sign whose function it is to identify the hero usurps the status of the hero. Instead of identifying Jack by means of the bag, Miss Prism identifies the bag by means of the "injury" that it received from a Gower Street omnibus—an injury that would appear to be a parodic allusion to the famous scar which shows Eurycleia whose feet she is washing (in both cases, two decades or more have passed when the hero re-encounters his nurse).

Parodies have a metaliterary tendency. By both imitating and distorting a text or a genre, they lay bare its conventions, pulling the audience out of the represented world and making it aware of the means and methods of representation. This is especially true of the anagnorisis of *The Importance of Being Earnest*. Wilde makes no attempt to hide the fact that he is using a literary convention. On the contrary, by offering an extremely ingenious and improbable solution to Jack's problems he highlights the contrived and artificial character of the convention. A metaliterary note is also struck by the curious replacement of a baby with a manuscript, of a child with a brainchild. While the manuscript obviously stands for literature, the baby represents life in its most pristine and natural form. When Miss Prism puts the former in the place of the latter, literature prevails over life. Perhaps we may even detect an allegory of parody in Miss Prism's mistake. After all, there are two contents and two containers: a baby who belongs in a pram, and a manuscript which belongs in a bag. Exchanging the baby and the manuscript brings about the very incongruity of form and content which is typical of parody. Be that as it may, the metaliterary quality of the anagnorisis is also suggested by the comments of the participants, who talk as if they knew that they are characters in a play. When Jack rushes off to search for the handbag, Lady Bracknell states that "strange coincidences are not supposed to occur" (3.369–70), and Gwendolen adds, "This suspense is terrible. I hope it will last" (3.378)—a paradoxical wish that combines the point of view of a character with that of a spectator.[6]

The way to the true anagnorisis is paved with a number of ludicrously false ones. After Miss Prism's assumption that the scene is about handbags rather than about human beings, Jack makes a discovery that is no less ridiculous:

Jack. (*in a pathetic voice*) Miss Prism, more is restored to you than this hand-
　　bag. I was the baby you placed in it.
Miss Prism. (*amazed*) You?
Jack. (*embracing her*) Yes—mother!
Miss Prism. (*recoiling in indignant astonishment*) Mr Worthing! I am
　　unmarried!
Jack. Unmarried! I do not deny that is a serious blow. But after all, who has
　　the right to cast a stone against one who has suffered? Cannot repen-
　　tance wipe out an act of folly? Why should there be one law for men,
　　and another for women? Mother, I forgive you. (*Tries to embrace her
　　again*)
Miss Prism. (*still more indignant*) Mr Worthing, there is some error. (*Point-
　　ing to Lady Bracknell*) There is the lady who can tell you who you really
　　are.
　　　(3.391–404).

Just as in the exchange about the handbag, moods and attitudes are singu-
larly mismatched. Jack feels all the emotions appropriate to an anagnorisis
scene. He is so full of joy and gratitude that he is moved to forgive his
mother for straying from the path of virtue. But Miss Prism, who has
maintained a rigid respectability throughout the play, is highly offended
by Jack's assumption that she has given birth to an illegitimate child. To
her, his generous words of forgiveness come as a gross insult. It should
be added that the exchange between Jack and Miss Prism amounts to an
exercise in self-parody on Wilde's part. It makes fun of the fallen woman,
a subject that he deals with in a serious manner in *Lady Windermere's
Fan* and *A Woman of No Importance*. Jack's speech is a comic echo of the
message of these earlier plays, including an almost verbatim repetition of
Hester's complaint about the double standard in *A Woman of No Importance*
(2.299–300).[7]

The scene in which Jack proposes to Gwendolyn provides us with
another interesting example of Wildean parody:

Jack. Gwendolen, I must get christened at once—I mean we must get married
　　at once. There is no time to be lost.

Gwendolen. Married, Mr Worthing?

Jack. (*astounded*) Well . . . surely. You know that I love you, and you led me to
believe, Miss Fairfax, that you were not absolutely indifferent to me.

Gwendolen. I adore you. But you haven't proposed to me yet. Nothing has
been said at all about marriage. The subject has not even been touched
on.

Jack. Well . . . may I propose to you now?

Gwendolen. I think it would be an admirable opportunity. And to spare
you any possible disappointment, Mr Worthing, I think it only fair to
tell you quite frankly beforehand that I am fully determined to accept
you.

Jack. Gwendolen!

Gwendolen. Yes, Mr Worthing, what have you got to say to me?

Jack. You know what I have got to say to you.

Gwendolen. Yes, but you don't say it.

Jack. Gwendolen, will you marry me? (*Goes on his knees*)

Gwendolen. Of course I will, darling. How long you have been about it! I am
afraid you have had very little experience in how to propose.

Jack. My own one, I have never loved anyone in the world but you.

Gwendolen. Yes, but men often propose for practice. I know my brother Ger-
ald does. All my girl-friends tell me so. What wonderfully blue eyes you
have, Ernest! They are quite, quite, blue. I hope you will always look at
me just like that, especially when there are other people present.
  (1.413–40)

Even more than in the anagnorisis scene, in which she and her mother
make comments with metadramatic overtones, Gwendolen thinks of the
occasion in terms of a script and of a part that has to be played and to be
practiced. In this case, the parodic incongruity does not result from a clash
between a high, dignified form and a low, ignoble content, but from the
contrast between Gwendolen's formal and artificial script and Jack's more
flexible and spontaneous one. He talks extempore, assuming that there is
no need to utter what has already been implied. Gwendolen, however, does
not tolerate any deviation from her script; she makes her suitor play his
part and say all his lines. Paradoxically, her very insistence on following
the script brings about a major deviation from it. In a proposal conducted
along traditional lines, it is the man who plays the active part, while the
woman reacts to his demands. In the case of Jack and Gwendolen, these
roles are exchanged. Not only is Gwendolen in charge of the conversation,
she even assumes that ultimate privilege of the male sex, the praise of the
beloved's eyes.[8]

A final parodic feature of the proposal and other exchanges between Jack and Gwendolen becomes evident if one compares them with similar scenes from the second courtship plot. I have already mentioned the way in which *The Importance of Being Earnest* parodies Wilde's treatment of the fallen woman in his previous works. In addition, the play offers something like a parody of itself, with later scenes or speeches providing comic repetitions of earlier ones. Jack's proposal to Gwendolen is replayed by Algernon and Cecily, with minor variations on the same themes. Cecily also confesses her fascination with the name "Ernest" (2.505); she also admires her lover's beauty—not his eyes, but his curls (2.489, 2.530)—and she also thinks of the proposal in terms of a script. In her case, this script is not merely a metaphorical or mental one; the story of her courtship by Algernon has literally been written down in her diary. The parodic effect of this has been pointed out by Neill Sammells, who makes a number of perceptive comments on Wildean parody in an essay on Tom Stoppard's *Travesties*:

> The structure of Wilde's play is that of a travesty: Jack's proposal to Gwendolen is played again, and travestied, by Algy and Cecily; Lady Bracknell's interrogation of Jack in Act One reappears in a different form in her haranguing of Miss Prism. Similarly, individual scenes are themselves structured by travesty with one voice restating and confounding the other. (383)

Sammells does not explain what he means by the latter kind of travesty based on "one voice restating and confounding the other" in a single scene, but the following exchange between Gwendolen and Cecily might qualify as an example. It is the quarrel that follows their mistaken discovery that they are both engaged to the same man:

Cecily. (*rather shy and confidingly*) Dearest Gwendolen, there is no reason why I should make a secret of it to you. Our little county newspaper is sure to chronicle the fact next week. Mr Ernest Worthing and I are engaged to be married.

Gwendolen. (*quite politely, rising*) My darling Cecily, I think there must be some slight error. Mr Ernest Worthing is engaged to me. The announcement will appear in the *Morning Post* on Saturday at the latest.

Cecily. (*very politely, rising*) I am afraid you must be under some misconception. Ernest proposed to me exactly ten minutes ago. (*Shows diary*)

Gwendolen. (*examines diary through her lorgnette carefully*) It is very curious, for he asked me to be his wife yesterday afternoon at 5.30. If you would care to verify the incident, pray do so. (*Produces diary of her own*) I never travel without my diary. One should always have something sensational to read in the train. I am so sorry, dear Cecily, if it is any disappointment to you, but I am afraid I have the prior claim.

Cecily. It would distress me more than I can tell you, dear Gwendolen, if it caused you any mental or physical anguish, but I feel bound to point out that since Ernest proposed to you he clearly has changed his mind.

Gwendolen. (*meditatively*) If the poor fellow has been entrapped into any foolish promise I shall consider it my duty to rescue him at once, and with a firm hand.

Cecily. (*thoughtfully and sadly*) Whatever unfortunate entanglement my dear boy may have got into, I will never reproach him with it after we are married.

(2.622–48)

Gwendolen and Cecily imitate each other to an extraordinary degree. They perform the same actions (showing a diary to their rival), strike the same attitudes ("*meditatively*" and "*thoughtfully*"), and say exactly the same things, a fact that is only highlighted by their elaborate efforts at finding synonyms: "some slight error"—"some misconception"; "I am so sorry"—"It would distress me"; "the poor fellow"—"my dear boy"; "entrapped"—"entanglement"; etc. The parodic effect is brought about in a rather unusual manner in this dialogue. It would be misleading to say that the speeches uttered by one woman are exaggerated, distorted or debased version of the speeches delivered by the other. Instead, the parodic effect results from the closeness of the imitation. Gwendolen and Cecily violate the assumption that human beings should be individuals, not Bergsonian parrots who repeat somebody else's words and actions. If there is an element of parodic debasing, it consists in this reduction of a human being to a puppet. At any rate, the repetitions across or within the scenes from the two courtship plots are similar to the more obvious examples of parody, such as the anagnorisis, in that they strongly emphasize the artificiality of the characters' words and actions; instead of being spontaneous and unpredictable, these are governed by prior scripts and models.

Before we move on to paradox, a final word needs to be said about the mode of parody in *The Importance of Being Earnest*. Parodies can be satiric; witness Henry Fielding's *Shamela*, which ridicules both the literary form and the social values of Samuel Richardson's *Pamela*. Richard Foster interprets *The Importance of Being Earnest* along these lines. He argues that "[b]y exposing and burlesquing the vacuities of a moribund literature Wilde satirizes, too, the society that sustains and produces it" (23). According to this view, the girls' romantic scripts, which they have imbibed from novels and plays and which they impose on their lovers, are bound up with hollow social values, and the parody of the literary conventions becomes a satiric attack on these values. In my view, however, the play's parody is ludic rather than satiric.[9] The parodic scenes discussed in this essay offer a lot of comic incongruity, but the laughter evoked by this incongruity is not directed at a particular target. It is not satiric laughter that attacks one set of values in the name of another. As Andreas Höfele argues, the play lacks a precondition of effective satire: a standpoint (191). In the proposal scenes, for instance, we laugh at the young women's infatuation with an artificial social ritual, but we also admire the energy and the inventiveness that they show in shaping this ritual. And we laugh at their lovers just as much as at the young women. It would be simplistic to argue that the proposal scenes ridicule formality and etiquette in order to endorse a more natural and spontaneous way of interacting with other human beings.

To clarify what I mean by ludic parody, it might be helpful to borrow a distinction from Wayne Booth's *Rhetoric of Irony*, a borrowing that seems to me justified because of the proximity of irony and parody. Both of these rhetorical strategies entail the assumption of a voice that is not one's own; in irony, this voice is usually an invented one that is created by the ironist him- or herself; in parody, it is borrowed from a prior text. Booth distinguishes between stable and unstable irony. Faced with stable irony, the audience notices that the speaker cannot possibly mean what he or she says, and it infers what is meant instead (usually the opposite of what has been said). Faced with unstable irony, the audience notices that the speaker cannot possibly mean what he or she says, but it is incapable of taking the second step, of concluding what is really meant; the speaker does not commit him- or herself to any particular meaning. If we apply this distinction to our topic, stable irony becomes the equivalent of satiric parody, while unstable irony becomes the equivalent of ludic parody. With satiric parody, the audience realizes that the parodist ridicules the parodied text and its values, and it infers what a more natural text and a saner set of values would look like. With ludic parody, the audience notices that there is some sort of comic incongruity (in other words, that there is parody), but finds itself incapable of taking the second step, of inferring a set of values and a text that could replace the parodied text and its values. The experience of watching or reading *The Importance of Being Earnest* is of the latter sort.

3. Paradox in Wilde

I have given a fairly extensive analysis of parody in *The Importance of Being Earnest* as this topic has not been discussed by many critics. The topic of paradox in this play and in Wilde's writings generally has received more attention;[10] thus it need not detain us very long. However, before moving on to the connection between parody and paradox we should consider a distinction between two types of paradox that is relevant to Wilde's use of this device. The first type links opposite terms in a contradictory manner, as in "less is more." Paradoxes of this sort are infrequent in Wilde. He prefers a second type, which consists in stating the opposite of a received opinion; in other words, this second type of paradox contradicts not itself but common sense.[11] An example is provided by Gwendolen. As the analysis of the proposal scene has shown, she has little respect for traditional gender roles. This also becomes evident in the following speech: "Outside the family circle, papa, I am glad to say, is entirely unknown. I think that is quite as it should be. The home seems to me to be the proper sphere for the man" (2.563–65). There is nothing self-contradictory about this speech; what it contradicts is the Victorian view that a wife should be the angel in the house, while her husband goes abroad to fight the battles of the world. A further example of the anti-commonsensical paradox comes from "The Decay of Lying," an essay that is in the tradition of the paradoxical encomium, a genre that praises what is normally dispraised." Wilde's praise of lying attacks a number of received ideas, in particular the nineteenth-century doctrine of realism. Whereas the realists argue that it is the task of art to imitate life, Wilde claims that the exact opposite is valid: "Life imitates Art far more than Art imitates Life" (239).

Furthermore, it should be kept in mind that a mere contradiction, of whatever kind, does not amount to a paradox. With both types of paradox, the element of contradiction has to be complemented by the possibility of sense. On the one hand, a paradox startles us with a violation of logic or common sense; on the other hand, it allows and challenges us to make sense of it, to endow absurdity with meaning. If this possibility of sense did not exist, we would not be dealing with a paradox but with mere error and inconsistency.

4. The Connection Between Parody and Paradox

Para means 'beside,' *ode* means 'song,' and *doxa* means 'opinion.' Literally, a parody is something that positions itself 'beside a song' (or, more generally, beside a text), whereas a paradox positions itself 'beside an opinion.' This etymological consideration suggests a first link. The text or opinion that parody or paradox responds to must be generally known. There is no point in positioning oneself beside something which no one is familiar with; if a parody or a paradox are to be recognized as such, the audience must be acquainted with the text or the opinion they are based on.

The preposition *para*, which is present in both terms, refers to the procedure that parody or paradox apply to a text or to an opinion. If we stick to the principal meaning of *para*, this procedure places parody 'beside a familiar text,' and paradox 'beside a received opinion.' In the case of paradox, 'beside' does not designate the concept with sufficient precision. The meaning has to be shifted to 'against' or 'contrary to.' For a paradox is not merely incongruous with a received opinion; it maintains the exact opposite. In the case of parody, the meaning of *para* cannot be narrowed down in a similar fashion. The preposition has a greater range of meaning as the techniques of parody are various: it can exaggerate the stylistic features of the parodied text, debase its content, or invert one of its elements, turning it into its opposite. In other words, a parody can place itself 'beside,' 'below,' or 'against' a text. Thus there is a partial overlap in the procedures of parody and paradox: inversion, or the change to the opposite, which amounts to the principal procedure of the latter, is at least one of the techniques of the former.

The main difference between the two terms is that between *ode* and *doxa*. A parody responds to a song or, more generally, a text, while a paradox responds to a received opinion. However, this difference is minimised if a received opinion is routinely expressed in a particular text, if text and opinion are so closely connected that a response to one entails a response to the other. A connection of this kind exists, for example, in proverbs and idioms, in which a commonsensical notion is coupled with a fixed expression. Interestingly, Wilde has a predilection for taking such an expression and replacing one of its words with its opposite.[13] What results is both a parody and a paradox. An example is provided by the following speech from *The Importance of Being Earnest*, in which Algernon anticipates the tedium of a dinner at Lady Bracknell's:

> She will place me next Mary Farquhar, who always flirts with her own husband across the dinner-table. That is not very pleasant. Indeed, it is not even decent . . . and that sort of thing is enormously on the increase. The amount of women in London who flirt with their own husbands is perfectly scandalous. It looks so bad. It is simply washing one's clean linen in public. (1.239–44)

Algernon parodies the idiom *to wash one's dirty linen in public* by performing a minimal formal change; he replaces the adjective *dirty* with its antonym *clean*. The resulting inversion of the idiom's meaning also produces a paradox. While common sense maintains that one should not publicise one's affairs and adulteries, Algernon thinks the same about marital happiness and harmony. He considers it "perfectly scandalous" for a couple to flaunt the lack of scandal in their marriage.

A second example of the combination of parody and paradox from *The Importance of Being Earnest* is slightly more complex. The received opinion that is targeted here is the notion that a person's social rank is reflected not merely in birth and possessions but also in his or her manners. The 'text' that expresses this opinion is not a fixed string of words but, more loosely, a convention in the characterization of masters and servants in comedy. In this genre, the masters drink, preferably wine or champagne, whereas the servants eat, usually fairly rich food.[14] Wilde brings about an exchange of these roles in the first scene of his play:

Algernon. [H]ave you got the cucumber sandwiches cut for Lady Bracknell?
Lane. Yes, sir. (*Hands them on a salver*)
Algernon. (*inspects them, takes two, and sits down on the sofa*) Oh! . . . by the way, Lane, I see from your book that on Thursday night, when Lord Shoreham and Mr Worthing were dining with me, eight bottles of champagne are entered as having been consumed.
Lane. Yes, sir; eight bottles and a pint.
Algernon. Why is it that at a bachelor's establishment the servants invariably drink the champagne? I ask merely for information.
Lane. I attribute it to the superior quality of the wine, sir. I have often observed that in married households the champagne is rarely of a first-rate brand.
Algernon. Good heavens! Is marriage so demoralizing as that?
Lane. I believe it is a very pleasant state, sir. I have had very little experience of it myself up to the present. I have only been married once. That was in consequence of a misunderstanding between myself and a young person.
Algernon. (*languidly*) I don't know that I am much interested in your family life, Lane.
Lane. No, sir; it is not a very interesting subject. I never think of it myself.
Algernon. Very natural, I am sure. That will do, Lane, thank you.
Lane. Thank you, sir. *Lane goes out*
Algernon. Lane's views on marriage seem somewhat lax. Really, if the lower orders don't set us a good example, what on earth is the use of them? They seem, as a class, to have absolutely no sense of moral responsibility.
    (1.8–36)

Wilde parodies the convention by inverting it. The servant drinks champagne, while the master eats voraciously.[15] By the time Lady Bracknell arrives, Algernon has devoured all of the cucumber sandwiches, and in a later scene he will make short work of the muffins served at Jack's country residence. The dialogue between Algernon and Lane nicely illustrates the closeness between parody and paradox in the play, as it culminates in a paradox which is also based on an inversion of the roles of master and servant. Whereas Victorian common sense regards it as a task of the middle and upper classes to set a good example to those lower down the social scale, Jack expects Lane to act as a role model for him: "Really, if the lower orders don't set us a good example, what on earth is the use of them?" One might retort that Lane is still useful to Algernon in serving the cucumber sandwiches, but such mundane considerations are foreign to Algernon, who shares his author's penchant for sweeping generalisation.

My final and most important argument for the connection between parody and paradox hinges on the concept of play. This concept has already been touched upon in the second section of this essay, where the mode of parody in *The Importance of Being Earnest* has been described as ludic. This ludic mode should not be confused with recreational drollery. It is not a temporary relaxation from (and thus subordinate to) seriousness. It is rather motivated by a fundamental uncertainty, by a scepticism that finds it difficult to take anything seriously. It is this mode of sceptical play which also characterizes Wilde's paradoxes—at least if we follow the author's own suggestions. Wilde offers us a theory of paradox in which the concept of play figures prominently. This theory is to be found in the first chapters of *The Picture of Dorian Gray*, and it is mainly associated with Lord Henry, Dorian's aristocratic mentor (and tempter). The following passage describes Lord Henry enchanting a dinner-table audience with his paradoxical rhetoric:

> "Nowadays most people die of a sort of creeping common sense, and discover when it is too late that the only things one never regrets are one's mistakes."
>
> A laugh ran round the table.
>
> He played with the idea, and grew wilful; tossed it into the air and transformed it; let it escape and recaptured it; made it iridescent with fancy, and winged it with paradox. The praise of folly, as he went on, soared into a philosophy, and Philosophy herself became young, and catching the mad music of Pleasure, wearing, one might fancy, her wine-stained robe and wreath of ivy, danced like a Bacchante over the hills of life, and mocked the slow Silenus for being sober. [...] It was an extraordinary improvisation.
>
> (78–79)

Lord Henry's rhetoric is essentially paradoxical. He starts out by disparaging common sense, the antagonist of paradox, and continues with the paradox that "the only thing one never regrets are one's mistakes." In his poetic description of Lord Henry's talk, the narrator mentions the term explicitly ("winged it with paradox"), and he also weaves the title of the most famous paradoxical encomium of world literature, Erasmus's *Praise of Folly*, into this description.[16] The terms used to characterize Lord Henry's paradoxical rhetoric emphasize its ludic quality. It is play and improvisation; instead of weighing and pondering his ideas, Lord Henry throws them into the air and juggles them. This intellectual play is slightly mad and inebriated, but it is also far from mere drollery and facetiousness. For all its folly, it maintains the rank of a philosophy.

Lord Henry's interlocutors frequently claim that he does not mean what he says, or they ask him whether his paradoxes are to be taken seriously (55, 76, 77, 80). He carefully avoids giving a straight answer to this question. If he answers in the affirmative, the ludic quality of the paradoxes will be eliminated. If he answers in the negative, the play will be at least diminished, framed and diminished by a context of seriousness. Lord Henry prefers a more radical kind of play, a play which includes seriousness at least as a possibility, which leaves its audience in the dark as to whether, and to what degree, it should be taken seriously. Here is how Lord Henry responds to Basil Hallward's charge that he lacks sincerity:

> "I don't agree with a single word that you have said, and, what is more, Harry, I feel sure you don't either."
>
> [. . .] "How English you are, Basil! That is the second time you have made that observation. If one puts forward an idea to a true Englishman—always a rash thing to do—he never dreams of considering whether the idea is right or wrong. The only thing he considers of any importance is whether one believes it oneself. Now, the value of an idea has nothing whatsoever to do with the sincerity of the man who expresses it. Indeed, the probabilities are that the more insincere the man is, the more purely intellectual will the idea be, as in that case it will not be coloured by either his wants, his desires, or his prejudices."
>
> (55)

Again, Lord Henry carefully avoids stating how serious he is about the claims he has made. Instead, he launches a surprising but not unpersuasive attack on the merits of seriousness and sincerity, thus giving a defence of the cognitive value of intellectual play.

In the following passage, we see two listeners responding to a paradox uttered by Lord Henry at his aunt's dinner table:

> "I can stand brute force, but brute reason is quite unbearable. There is something unfair about its use. It is hitting below the intellect."
> "I do not understand you," said Sir Thomas, growing rather red.
> "I do, Lord Henry," murmured Mr Erskine, with a smile.
> "Paradoxes are all very well in their way . . ." rejoined the Baronet.
> "Was that a paradox?" asked Mr Erskine. "I did not think so. Perhaps it was. Well, the way of paradoxes is the way of truth."
> (77)

The first response comes from Sir Thomas, the advocate of common sense. At first he finds Lord Henry's remark so absurd that he fails to understand it; then he grudgingly concedes that it might qualify as a paradox. But the manner in which he phrases this admission—"paradoxes are all very well in *their* way"—indicates that he considers them an aberration from the path of reason and virtue. To him, paradox is a frivolous and inferior mode of speech that should not be admitted into postprandial conversation, let alone into serious intellectual debate. The second response comes from Mr Erskine, introduced by the narrator as a "gentleman of considerable charm and culture" (76). Mr Erskine does not find Lord Henry's remark absurd. He does not even regard it as a paradox; so convincing does it appear to him. Then he admits, like Sir Thomas but from a very different point of view, that it might be considered a paradox, but he hastens to add that paradoxes lead towards truth. Mr Erskine picks up the image of the way introduced by Sir Thomas, an image that implies movement, and his own response is significantly dynamic, characterized by a to and fro. Lord Henry's paradox has set Mr Erskine's mind in motion. This is, on the listener's part, the same intellectual motion that also characterizes the rhetorical play of paradox on the speaker's part, a kind of play that embraces seriousness as one possibility among others.[17]

I would like to make a final stab at defining the ludic mode discussed here by looking at the pun on which the comedy ends. As it plays with a word that refers to the opposite of play, it has an obvious bearing on the present discussion:

Lady Bracknell. My nephew, you seem to be displaying signs of triviality.
  Jack. On the contrary, Aunt Augusta, I've now realized for the first time in my life the vital Importance of Being Earnest.

The form of the final sentence conveys the exact opposite of its content. The ludic manner in which it states the vital importance of being earnest amounts to an assertion of the vital importance of not being earnest. Because of this combination of opposites, it amounts to a kind of paradox and provides another example of the link between paradox and play that I have discussed with respect to Lord Henry's rhetoric. In playing with the word "Earnest," the final pun repeats what the entire play has done with the name "Ernest" and the concept of seriousness. Throughout the comedy, Ernest is only played: it is a fiction invented by Jack, a role used by him and Algernon, a fantasy embellished by Gwendolen and Cecily. When the final twist of the plot reveals that Jack's name is Ernest after all, it does so in the same spirit of parodic play that we have seen at work in the earlier stages of the anagnorisis, such as the recovery of a long-lost handbag. "Earnest" may be the final word of the comedy, but only according to the letter; according to the spirit, the final word is play.

5. Why Is *The Importance of Being Earnest* Wilde's Masterpiece?

The Importance of Being Earnest is generally considered Wilde's supreme achievement. Some critics have justified this view by arguing that in his earlier plays, and in *Dorian Gray*, the sophisticated rhetoric of such characters as Lord Henry, Mrs Erlynne or Lord Illingworth is at odds with other elements of the work, whereas in *The Importance of Being Earnest* this rhetoric is part of a coherent whole.[18] Erika Meier describes the artistic discrepancy in the early plays as a clash between witty dialogue and melodramatic plot. Only in his final play does Wilde succeed in fusing action and dialogue:

> The surprising events find their counterpart in the unexpectedness of the epigrams; the plot, with its final ironic twist, is complemented by the innumerable paradoxical sayings; and the parallel development of the action (the romance of Gwendolen and Jack on the one hand and of Cecily and Algernon on the other hand) corresponds to the formal and often symmetrical dialogue. In his last play Wilde indeed succeeded in fusing the drama of language (as created in his earlier works) and the drama of action. (195)[19]

I find myself in basic agreement with Meier's claims. In fact, the present essay provides an explanation of how "the plot [...] is complemented by the innumerable paradoxical sayings." It is because the treatment of the plot is parodic, and because of the links between parody and paradox pointed out above, that *The Importance of Being Earnest* is all of a piece. In the earlier plays and in *Dorian Gray*, the plot is treated in a serious or even melodramatic fashion; these works lack the coherence between parody and paradox that characterizes Wilde's last play.

The incompatibility between playful paradoxes and a serious plot in the earlier works is illustrated by the ending of *Dorian Gray*. In this novel, the protagonist and his portrait change places in the first chapters. The man remains pure and beautiful like a work of art, whereas the picture turns more and more hideous with every evil act that Dorian commits. When he finally attempts to destroy the portrait, wishing to eliminate the visual record of his sins, he brings about his own death. Portrait and protagonist change places again; the former regains its original beauty, while the latter turns into an ugly and withered corpse. Thus the ending of the novel depicts a punishment of sin; it underlines the allegorical and cautionary character of the plot, whose orthodox morality and seriousness are a far cry from the exuberant and playful scepticism of Lord Henry's paradoxes.

The incompatibility between the plot and the paradoxes of *Dorian Gray* is not merely a matter of mode and atmosphere; there are even more specific contradictions between them. At one point, Lord Henry states:

> The mutilation of the savage has its tragic survival in the self-denial that mars our lives. We are punished for our refusals. Every impulse that we strive to strangle broods in the mind, and poisons us. The body sins once, and has done with its sin, for action is a mode of purification. [...] The only way to get rid of a temptation is to yield to it. (61–62)

Whereas common sense maintains that we keep morally pure by resisting temptation and avoiding sin, Lord Henry claims that the opposite is true. Self-denial poisons; sinning purifies. The plot, however, does not follow this paradoxical logic. Every temptation that Dorian yields to leaves its mark on the portrait; every sin that he commits adds another blemish. It is only in Lord Henry's speech that action is a mode of purification; in the plot of the novel, it remains a mode of defilement. The plot also clashes with the paradoxes of "The Decay of Lying" mentioned in the third section of this essay. Admittedly, there is a temporary period in which these paradoxes seem to govern the plot. After the man and the portrait have changed places, life does imitate art in that Dorian is and remains as beautiful as the picture of his younger self. But in the portrait the traditional principles of mimesis and morality are upheld; art imitates life and teaches an ethical lesson in that every sin committed by Dorian is mirrored in the painting. It is the logic of the portrait that prevails in the end. Dorian's self-fashioning fails; the beautiful lie that his life is built on collapses, while the ugly truth is revealed. To sum up, the ending of *Dorian Gray* is at odds with the paradoxical rhetoric in this novel and in "The Decay of Lying," and this discrepancy remains unresolved.

The ending of *The Importance of Being Earnest* is comparable to the ending of *Dorian Gray* in that it also concerns the identity of the protagonist and his relationship with a kind of *doppelgänger* that enables him to lead a double life. In the novel, the *doppelgänger* is the miraculously changing image that inhabits the picture painted by Basil Hallward. This image allows Dorian to lead a life of sin because it bears the marks of this life, thus making it possible for him to appear spotless and innocent in the eyes of the world. The ending of the novel shows the tragic folly of this double life; the *doppelgänger* is annihilated when the picture returns to its former status as an ordinary portrait that is no longer subject to miraculous change. The *doppelgänger* of the play is "Ernest," the role that Jack has invented for the time he spends in London; this *doppelgänger* is surprisingly confirmed by the ending. It is revealed that Jack has indeed been christened "Ernest"; he has invented the truth, as it were. Of course, this confirmation is given in the same spirit of parodic play that characterizes the entire anagnorisis up to the final pun; the *doppelgänger* is confirmed precisely because he, too, is a manifestation of playing. Thus the ending does not amount to a lapse into seriousness; it is informed by the ludic mode that also inspires the paradoxical rhetoric of the play. The ending is also in tune with the very paradoxes of "The Decay of Lying"[20] that are negated by the ending of *Dorian Gray*. In *The Importance of Being Earnest*, life imitates art in that "Ernest," the creative lie, turns out to be true. The role is the ultimate reality; the truest poetry is the most feigning.

NOTES

1. The first version of this essay was delivered at the *Connotations* Symposium on "Sympathetic Parody," which took place in Mettlach and Saarbrücken in late July 2003. I am grateful to Matthias Bauer for organising this event, which was a felicitous combination of *prodesse* and *delectare*, and to the participants for their responses to my talk. I should also like to express my gratitude to Maik Goth, Frank Kearful, Sven Wagner and the anonymous *Connotations* reviewers for their comments on earlier drafts of this essay.

2. To the best of my knowledge, this connection has not been systematically explored. In "Raymond Chandler: Burlesque, Parody, Paradox," Winifred Crombie analyses the links between clauses in Chandler's prose; she touches upon paradox only in the rather remote sense of inter-clausal connections of an illogical Lurid. She also claims that Chandler parodies the genre of detective fiction, but fails to establish a connection between parody and paradox.

3. See *Poetics* 1454b.

4. A particularly lachrymose example is the anagnorisis in Richard Steele's *The Conscious Lovers* (5.3), in which the merchant Sealand is reunited with his long-lost daughter Indiana.

5. See, for instance, Abrams 26, and Genette 19.

6. There is an additional metadramatic comment in the original four-act version, which Wilde cut at the behest of the director, George Alexander. After Jack has left the scene to search for the handbag, Lady Bracknell says, rather like an Aristotelian drama critic, "I sincerely hope nothing improbable is going to happen. The improbable is always in bad, or at any rate, questionable taste." See *The Original Four-Act Version of The Importance of Being Earnest* 105.

7. This parodic self-echo is also pointed out by Meier 190 and Gregor 512–13.

8. Female dominance is not limited to the proposal scene or the relationship between Gwendolen and Jack; it characterizes all of the heterosexual relationships in the play, and some others elsewhere in Wilde's oeuvre. In *The Picture of Dorian Gray*, for instance, Lord Henry gossips about a forward American heiress who "has made up her mind to propose" to Lord Dartmoor (76). On female dominance in *The Importance of Being Earnest*, see Kohl, *Das literarische Werk* 176–77, Parker 176–77, and Raby 63.

9. I borrow the term *ludic* from Gerard Genette's typology of parody and its related modes. One of Genette's distinctions concerns the attitude that a text may take towards the text(s) that it transforms or imitates. There are three basic modes: first, a satirical or polemical mode in which the source text is ridiculed; second, a ludic mode which creates comic tension between the two texts but no ridicule or derision at the expense of the source; third, a serious mode that translates a text into another genre or cultural context without any comic distortion (33–37). An example of the first mode is Henry Fielding's *Shamela*, of the second (as I would like to claim), *The Importance of Being Earnest*, of the third, Thomas Mann's *Doktor Faustus*. In his important article on parody and comedy, Ian Donaldson makes a distinction which is similar to the distinction between the first two of Genette's modes: "[M]uch of our delight in watching a comedy comes from our recognition of the presence of time-honoured situations, complications, and resolutions, which are introduced in a spirit not so much of ridicule or burlesque as of playful affection. The kind of comic parody which I want to explore [. . .] is not the open and sustained parody of the better-known burlesque and rehearsal plays, but a parody altogether more genial and gentle, devoid of major satirical intent, playing wryly but nonetheless delightedly with the conventions of the comic form" (45). I am grateful to Ian Donaldson for sending me a copy of his instructive article, which I had difficulties in obtaining.

10. See, for instance, Catsiapis, Hess-Lüttich, Naassar and Zeender.

11. On the differences between these two types of paradox and on their ultimate similarity, see Niederhoff 49–52.

12. On this genre, see Henry Knight Miller and Niederhoff 50–52, where further studies of the genre are listed.

13. For further examples of this technique, see Donaldson 45 and Ogala 228–29.

14. Some examples of servants who like to eat: Sosia in the various versions of *Amphitryon*; Dromio of Ephesus, who advises the man whom he believes to be his master, "Methinks your maw, like mine, should be your clock, / And strike you

home without a messenger" (*The Comedy of Errors* 1.2.66–67); Jeremy, who, in the opening scene of William Congreve's *Love for Love*, prefers real food to the nourishment of the mind. The link between masters and wine is shown by Congreve's Mellefont who is praised as "the very Essence of Wit, and Spirit of Wine" (*The Double-Dealer* 1.1.34–35), or by Sheridan's Charles and Careless who see it as "the great Degeneracy of the Age" that some of their fellows do not drink, that "they give into all the Substantial Luxuries of the Table—and abstain from nothing but wine and wit" (*The School for Scandal* 3.3.1–5). Another case in point is the debate about the respective merits of wine and women, a debate frequently conducted by young gentlemen in comedy (e.g. by Merryman and Cunningham in Charles Sedley's *Bellamira*); the debate is never about food and women.

15. This inversion of roles is missed by James M. Ware in his article on Algernon's appetite; Ware relates this appetite to the hedonism of the rakes in Restoration comedy.

16. This allusion may be more than a passing reference; it may indicate an influence of Erasmus on Wilde or at least a profound affinity between them. *The Praise of Folly* evinces some very close similarities to Wilde's writings and to *The Importance of Being Earnest* in particular. First, it draws on the literary traditions of both parody and the paradoxical encomium, as C. A. Patrides points out in an article on Erasmus and Thomas More (39). Second, the preface asserts that "[n]othing is more puerile, certainly, than to treat serious matters triflingly; but nothing is more graceful than to handle light subjects in such a way that you seem to have been anything but trifling" (3). This seems fairly close to the subtitle of Wilde's play, *A Trivial Comedy for Serious People*. Third, *The Praise of Folly* is also informed by a spirit of sceptical play, by the eschewal of a fixed position. As Patrides writes, "Erasmus's mercurial protagonist is wont to disavow a number of specifically Erasmian tenets, admit as many others, and—more often than not—disavow and admit them at once" (40).

17. The present explanation of the ludic quality of Wilde's paradoxes consists in a commentary on some passages from *The Picture of Dorian Gray*. Elsewhere I have given a more technical analysis of the ludic paradox, which distinguishes it from the comico-satirical paradox on the one hand, and the serious paradox on the other. This distinction is based on the relative weight of the opposites linked in a paradox, on the relative weight of the two principles which are at work in a paradox (contradiction and sense), and on the attitude taken by the speaker; see Niederhoff 60–76.

18. Ian Gregor claims that Wilde found a fitting dramatic environment for the dandy only in his final play but not in the earlier ones, a claim that is echoed in Raby 34. Norbert Kohl takes a similar view of the earlier plays: "Der grelle Kontrast zwischen Pathos und Paradoxon, zwischen der unvermittelten sprachlichen Melodramatik rührseliger Heroinen und dens artifiziellen Idiom der Dandys resultiert in Disharmonien, die der ästhetischen Homogenität der Stücke nicht eben zuträglich sind" (*Leben und Werk* 189).

19. See also Dariusz Pestka, who argues that in the early plays "the plot is not comic at all, and only verbal wit and a few amusing characters counterbalance the serious problems; whereas in the latter [*The Importance of Being Earnest*] the plot contributes to the playful mood and reinforces other comic devices" (191).

20. A link between this essay and the play is also established by E. B. Partridge in his article, "The Importance of Not Being Earnest."

Works Cited

Abrams, Meyer Howard. *A Glossary of Literary Terms*. 7th ed. Boston: Heinle & Heinle, 1999.

Aristotle. *Poetics: Classical Literary Criticism*. Eds. D. A. Russell and M. Winterbottom. The World's Classics. Oxford: OUP, 1989. 51–90.

Booth, Wayne C. *A Rhetoric of Irony*. Chicago: U of Chicago P, 1974.

Catsiapis, Hélène. "Ironie et paradoxes dans les comédies d'Oscar Wilde: une interprétation." *Thalia: Studies in Literary Humor* 1 (1978): 35–53.

Congreve, William. *The Complete Plays*. Ed. Herbert Davis. Chicago: U of Chicago P, 1967.

Crombie, Winifred. "Raymond Chandler: Burlesque, Parody, Paradox." *Language and Style: An International Journal* 16 (1983): 151–68.

Donaldson, Ian. "'The Ledger of the Lost-and-Stolen Office': Parody in Dramatic Comedy." *Southern Review: Literary and Interdisciplinary Essays* 13 (1980): 41–52.

Erasmus, Desiderius. *The Praise of Folly*. Ed. Hoyt Hopewell Hudson. New York: Random House, 1970.

Foster, Richard. "Wilde as Parodist: A Second Look at *The Importance of Being Earnest*." *College English* 18 (1956–57): 18–23.

Genette, Gérard. *Palimpsestes: La littérature au second degré*. Paris: Seuil, 1982.

Gregor, Ian. "Comedy and Oscar Wilde." *Sewanee Review* 74 (1966): 501–21.

Hess-Lüttich, Ernest W. B. "Die Strategie der Paradoxie: Zur Logik der Konversation im Dandyismus am Beispiel Oscar Wildes." *Semiotics of Drama and Theatre: New Perspectives in the Theory of Drama and Theatre*. Eds. Herta Sehmid and Aloysius van Kesteren. Amsterdam: Benjamins, 1984. 197–234.

Höfele, Andreas. *Parodie und literarischer Wandel: Studien zur Function einer Schreibweise in der englischen Literatur des ausgehenden 19. Jahrhunderts*. Heidelberg: Winter, 1986.

Kohl, Norbert. *Oscar Wilde: Leben und Werk*. Frankfurt a.M.: Insel, 2000.

———. *Oscar Wilde. Das literarische Werk zwischen Provokation und Anpassung*. Heidelberg: Winter, 1980.

Meier, Erika. *Realism and Reality: The Function of the Stage Directions in the New Drama from Thomas William Robertson to George Bernard Shaw*. Bern: Francke, 1967.

Miller, Henry Knight. "The Paradoxical Encomium with Special Reference to Its Vogue in England, 1600–1800." *Modern Philology* 53 (1955): 145–78.

Naassar, Christopher S. "On Originality and Influence: Oscar Wilde's Technique." *Journal of the Eighteen Nineties Society* 24 (1997): 37–47.

Niederhoff, Burkhard. *"The Rule of Contrary": Das Paradox in tier englischen Komödie der Restaurationszeit und des frühen 18. Jahrhunderts*. Trier: Wissenschaftlicher Verlag Trier, 2001.

Ogala, Aatos. *Aestheticism and Oscar Wilde*. 2 vols. Helsinki: n.p., 1955.

Parker, David. "Oscar Wilde's Great Farce." *Wilde: Comedies: A Casebook*. Ed. William Tydeman. London: Macmillan, 1982. 166–79.

Partridge, E. B. "The Importance of Not Being Earnest." *Bucknell Review* 9 (1960): 143–58.

Patrides, C. A. "Erasmus and More: Dialogues with Reality." *Kenyon Review* 8 (1986): 34–48.

Pestka, Dariusz. "A Typology of Oscar Wilde's Comic Devices." *Studia Anglica Posnaniensia: An International Review of English Studies* 22 (1989): 175–93.

Raby, Peter. *The Importance of Being Earnest: A Reader's Companion*. New York: Twayne, 1995.

Sammells, Neill. "Earning Liberties: *Travesties* and *The Importance of Being Earnest*." *Modern Drama* 29 (1986): 376–87.

Shakespeare, William. *The Complete Works*. Ed. Stanley Wells et al. Oxford: Clarendon P, 1986.

Sheridan, Richard Brinsley. *Sheridan's Plays*. Ed. Cecil Price. Oxford: OUP, 1975.

Ware, James M. "Algernon's Appetite: Oscar Wilde's Hero as Restoration Dandy." *English Literature in Transition* 13 (1970): 17–26.

Wilde, Oscar. *The Importance of Being Earnest and Other Plays*. Ed. Peter Raby. Oxford World's Classics. Oxford: OUP, 1995.

———. *The Major Works*. Ed. Isobel Murray. Oxford World's Classics. Oxford: OUP, 2000.

———. *The Original Four-Act Version of The Importance of Being Earnest: A Trivial Comedy for Serious People*. Ed. Vyvyan Holland. London: Methuen, 1957.

Zeender, Marie-Noelle. "Oscar Wilde: Le jeu du paradoxe." *Cycnos* 10 (1993): 53–61.

JAMES G. NELSON

"The Honey of Romance":
Oscar Wilde as Poet and Novelist

Among the attractive young men of the Old Testament is King Saul's son, Jonathan, remembered, perhaps, most for his love for and friendship with David, but also for his transgression of his father's interdict: "Cursed be the man that eateth any food until evening, that I may be avenged on mine enemies." Not having heard Saul's oath, Jonathan, as readers of the Bible may recall, soon after passed through a wood where there was honey on the ground. And in the words of the Old Testament, he "put forth the end of the rod that was in his hand, and dipped it in a honeycomb, and put his hand to his mouth; and his eyes were enlightened." Condemned to die by an unforgiving father, Jonathan, in words which were to have a curious attraction for some later Victorians, replied: "I did but taste a little honey with the end of the rod that was in mine hand, and, lo, I must die."[1]

How symbolic this incident must have been to the romantic poet, William Blake, who surely saw it as yet another biblical embodiment of the struggle between the youthful Ore, the voice of desire and rebellion, and the aged Urizen, the principle of tyranny and obedience unto the Law. Later, it was the metaphoric (and, perhaps, onanistic) implications of Jonathan's words which stirred the imagination of Walter Pater who associated Jonathan's honey and his enlightenment with all and even more than Matthew Arnold's Hellenism

From *Redefining the Modern: Essays on Literature and Society in Honor of Joseph Wiesenfarth*, edited by William Baker and Ira B. Nadel, pp. 130–47. Copyright © 2004 by Rosemont Publishing and Printing.

encompassed—in particular, the desire for physical beauty, the life of the senses, and the search for sensations.

In his essay on Wincklemann, which in 1873 was published as part of *Studies in the History of the Renaissance*, Pater, in calling attention to the ascetic bent of Christianity, its antagonism to "the artistic life, with its inevitable sensuousness," quoted with consummate effect Jonathan's words: "I did but taste a little honey with the end of the rod that was in mine hand, and, lo! I must die,"[2] thus enshrining David's passionate young companion as one of the saints of aestheticism who had fought the good fight in the cause of beauty.

This act of canonization was not lost upon one of Pater's earliest and most devoted followers, Oscar Wilde, who in the sonnet which he chose to preface his *Poems* of 1881, "Hélas!," associated his life with that of Jonathan's. Bemoaning the fact that he already had "given away" his "ancient wisdom, and austere control" in order to, in true aesthetic fashion, "drift with every passion till my soul / Is a stringed lute on which all winds can play," Wilde climaxed his poem with a paraphrase of Jonathan's poignant words:

> lo! with a little rod
> I did but touch the honey of romance—
> And must I lose a soul's inheritance?[3]

With his predilection for Arnold's "sweetness" and Pater's "honey," Wilde could hardly fail to have read in Jonathan's fateful history his own, given as he was to that sense of doom which readers of his work discern. Indeed, Jonathan's appetite for honey and, consequently, his inevitable clash with the Hebraic spirit embodied in Saul,[4] is the history not only of Wilde but of so many of his central characters. His desire for beauty, his ideal of self-realization through pleasure, his devotion to the life of the senses was to set him at every turn in opposition to the restrictive nature and ascetic bent of the Judaeo-Christian tradition. And although he was to flirt with the Roman Catholic church, pose as the guilt-ridden penitent, and imitate the life of Christ, Wilde genuinely was, like his poetic forebear, John Keats, a pagan, the exponent of an aesthetic creed and philosophic ideal hostile in the extreme to Christianity and the established paternalistic/patriarchal culture of his times.

If we can read his early poems as a reflection, at least in part, of his concerns as a young Oxford undergraduate, Wilde already had experienced the struggle between his pagan desires and his Christian conscience.[5] A trip to Italy in 1875 evidently brought on his first flirtation with Roman Catholicism which resulted in yet a second trip to Rome the following year and an audience with the Pope. Back at Oxford, he hung his walls at Magdalen with, among other things, photographs of the Holy Father and Cardinal Manning. Yet of symbolic significance is a further trip to Italy in 1877 which concluded with an excursion to Greece under the aegis of his old Trinity College, Dublin, professor of classics, John Mahaffy. Perhaps alarmed by Wilde's dalliance with Rome, Mahaffy, who had trained Wilde to be an excellent Greek scholar, told his pupil that he intended to make "an honest pagan out of" him.[6]

That Mahaffy's intentions were realized is suggested by the fact that the "Rosa Mystica" section of *Poems*, which is devoted primarily to Wilde's Italian journeys and his attraction to Roman Catholicism, concludes with "The New Helen," a poem which intimates the demise of Christianity and celebrates the rebirth of the worship of beauty in the form of Helen.[7] If Wilde did not intend for "The New Helen" to serve as his final thought on religious matters—at least for a time—one wonders why he deliberately chose to conclude the "Rosa Mystica" section with it. For the religion of suffering which he celebrated in the previous poems is clearly rejected in "The New Helen" in favor of a symbolic embodiment of the preeminence of fleshly beauty and the pleasures of the senses. If after all of his posturings, the young Wilde had failed to bend the knee to the Christian God, here he dedicates himself with fervor to his newly deified Helen, the latest (after Keats's Psyche) Olympian: "Yet care I not what ruin time may bring," he cries in words which were to prove prophetic, "if in thy temple thou wilt let me kneel" (108, ll. 59–60).

A kind of Swinburnean femme fatale, Wilde's Helen has been hiding out with Aphrodite "in that hollow hill"—presumably that Venusberg in Bavaria—while her Christian counterpart, Mary, Queen of Heaven—"Who gat from Love no joyous gladdening, / But only Love's intolerable pain" (108, ll. 47–48)—has been receiving the world's obeisance. Now, however, Helen has returned

> . . . our darkness to illume:
> For we, close-caught in the wide nets of Fate,
>   Wearied with waiting for the World's Desire,
>   Aimlessly wandered in the House of gloom,
> Aimlessly sought some slumberous anodyne
>   For wasted lives, for lingering wretchedness,
> Till we beheld thy re-arisen shrine,
>   And the white glory of thy loveliness.
>   (109, ll. 93–100)

The pagan virtues which Wilde's Helen represents and the enthusiasm with which he celebrates them are central to a number of other early poems in

which the bright sensuous landscapes and idyllic pleasures of Greek paganism
are played off against the gray, ugly, materialistic, puritanical world of the
present. In such longer poems as "The Garden of Eros," "Panthea," and "The
Burden of Itys," Wilde plays upon themes which, though largely unoriginal,
clearly are close to his heart. And although his penchant for mythmaking and
his zest for sensuous paganism remind one inevitably of Keats's early poetry,
especially "I Stood Tip-toe" and "Sleep and Poetry," the evident joy and ease
with which he writes reminds one that the most convincing portions of his
poetry and prose are those in which the pagan element—so often exploited
by A.C. Swinburne—is given full expression.

Having dedicated himself to "the Spirit of Beauty" in "The Garden of
Eros," and having assured her that there are still "a few" who have "in thy tem-
ples found a goodlier feast / Than this starved age can give" (131, ll. 112–13),
Wilde in "The Burden of Itys" voices his genuine hope that Beauty somehow
can triumph and bring back an age of pagan freedom and joy:

> Sing on! Sing on! Let the dull world grow young,
>   Let elemental things take form again,
> And the old shapes of Beauty walk among
>   The simple garths and open crofts, . . .
>   (62, ll. 169–72)

And in "Panthea," he enunciates fully (despite the Swinburnesque garb
and Paterian sentiments) the ideas about the life of sensations and the pursuit
of pleasure upon which he was, in time, to put his own stamp as they found
expression in, among other works, his literary criticism and his novel, *The
Picture of Dorian Gray*. Assuming a Rubáiyát-like stance toward life, Wilde
forbids his companion to trouble herself with "idle questions": "Nay," he goes
on to urge, "let us walk from fire unto fire, / From Passionate pain to dead-
lier delight" (110, ll. 1–2); and voicing sentiments Lord Henry Wotton later
might have repeated to Dorian Gray—"For, sweet, to feel is better than to
know"—the poet declares:

> One pulse of passion—youth's first fiery glow,—
>   Are worth the hoarded proverbs of the sage:
> Vex not thy soul with dead philosophy,
> Have we not lips to kiss with, hearts to love, and eyes to see!
>   (110, ll. 7, 9–12)

Like Lord Henry who in the novel will urge the Paterian philosophy of
the moment on Dorian, Wilde in "Panthea" views life essentially as "One

fiery-coloured moment: one great love; and lo! we die" (113, l. 84). So lived, life after death will be an eternal oneness with "all sensuous life" (114, l. 146).

The early poems not only embody in imitative form their author's pagan attitudes, but also provide us with our first acquaintance with the figure or image which is to become the central focus of Wilde's work. For example, this figure is appealingly embodied as the hero in what is supposed to be the poet's favorite poem, the early, rather Keatsian narrative romance entitled "Charmides." Named for the exceedingly beautiful and charming youth in Plato's early dialogue, "Charmides," Wilde's hero has the beauty and the youth but significantly lacks the central quality debated in the dialogue, namely, *sophrosyne*, roughly translated as moderation, self-control over one's physical appetites. A projection in art of Wilde's pagan self, Charmides is a "Grecian lad" of godlike beauty whose type is to blossom into the progressively more fully realized characters of Wilde's later works, above all, Dorian Gray whose handsome features are those of Charmides: "finely curved scarlet lips," "frank blue eyes," "crisp gold hair," and what Lord Henry describes as "all youth's passionate purity."[8]

Summing up within himself all those deeply romantic elements and pagan impulses which ruled the inner life of Wilde, Charmides is narcissistic, daring, a worshiper of beauty, and a passionate seeker of sensual pleasure. A youthful Greek mariner, Charmides, having returned from Sicily with his galley laden with "pulpy figs and wine," sets forth on a daring quest. Making his way at evening to the temple of Athena, he secretes himself within its precincts until all the priests and people have gone. When "through the open roof above the full and brimming moon / Flooded with sheeny waves the marble floor" of the temple, "the venturous lad" left his hiding place and flung wide "the cedar-carven door" which revealed Athena, "an awful image saffron-clad / And armed for battle!" (72, ll. 60–65). With total disregard for the sanctities of such a holy shrine and "ready for death," the audacious lad stood "well content at such a price to see / That calm wide brow, that terrible maidenhood, / The marvel of that pitiless chastity" (73, ll. 91–94). And despite the fact that "the twelve Gods leapt up in marble fear" and "on the frieze the prancing horses neighed" (73, ll. 86, 89), Charmides, his passion for the goddess fully aroused by her lovely form,

> . . . nigher came, and touched her throat, and with hands violate
> Undid the cuirass, and the crocus gown,
>   And bared the breasts of polished ivory,
> Till from the waist the peplos falling down
>   Left visible the secret mystery

Which to no lover will Athena show,
The grand cool flanks, the crescent thighs, the
   bossy hills of snow.
      (73, ll. 102–8)

Resting his "greedy eyes" on the "burnished image, till mere sight / Half swooned for surfeit of such luxuries," the lad, "his passion's will" unchecked, "flung his arms" about "the towered neck" while "his lips in hungering delight / Fed on her lips" (74, ll. 109–14). In what must be one of the strangest, albeit passionate, trysts in literature, Charmides spends the night with this image of Athena, never drawing "his lips from hers till overhead the lark of warning flew" (74, l. 126).

Needless to say, this act characterizes Charmides as a fearless youth whose curiosity about secret knowledge and whose desire for beauty and erotic pleasure prod him to a deed of daring and defiance as monumental as those of Faust and Prometheus. Like the young mariner in Coleridge's famous "Rime," Charmides sets himself apart from his fellows by his act of sacrilege which at once opens his eyes and seals his doom. Flying in the face of established taboos, he gazes upon "the secret mystery" of Athena, an enlightenment and act of passion for which he pays with his life.

Athena's beauties are not the only center of Charmides' attention, however. All beauty being but a reflection of his own, one is not surprised when, leaving Athena's shrine, Charmides seeks out "a little stream, which well he knew" (74, l. 139) where

   . . . down amid the startled reeds he lay
Panting in breathless sweet affright, and waited for the day.
On the green bank he lay, and let one hand
   Dip in the cool dark eddies listlessly,
And soon the breath of morning came and fanned
   His hot flushed cheeks, or lifted wantonly
The tangled curls from off his forehead, while
He on the running water gazed with strange and secret smile.
      (75, ll. 143–50)

Although some shepherds who pass by take Charmides to be either "young Hylas" or "young Dionysos," others, more perceptive, recognize in his beauty as well as in his streamside pose, the classic features of Narcissus, that lovely lad whom Ovid in *Metamorphoses* had made the androgynous son of a nymph and a river-god: "It is Narcissus," they cry, "his own paramour, / Those are the fond and crimson lips no woman can allure" (75, ll. 167–68).

While the following evening his mariners on shipboard cringe in fear, Charmides, "the over-bold adulterer, / A dear profaner of great mysteries, / An ardent amorous idolater," with ecstatic joy and the cry of "I come" on his lips, plunges into the sea to join the vengeful Athena, who lures "her boy lover" to his death (78, ll. 253–55, 257, 264).

Washed ashore on a Greek isle, Charmides' body is feared by all "save one white girl, who deemed it would not be / So dread a thing to feel a sea-god's arms / Crushing her breasts in amorous tyranny" (80, ll. 343–45). The white girl, especially her salient features—innocent purity allied with sensual passion—reminds one of Byron's Haidee, whose relationship with the young Juan is faintly paralleled here, and prefigures Sibyl Vane, whose fatal love for Dorian Gray, in the novel of that title, also centers in an impossible object.

Bound by an oath to Artemis, the white girl, nevertheless, has little use for what she refers to as her "pallid chastity"; thus overwhelmed by passion and desire for the object of her love, she offends the virgin huntress who, as vengeful as Athena, slays her.

> Sobbing her life out with a bitter cry,
>   On the boy's body fell the Dryad maid,
> Sobbing for incomplete virginity,
>   And raptures unenjoyed, and pleasures dead,
>   And all the pain of things unsatisfied,
> And the bright drops of crimson youth crept down
>   her throbbing side.
>   (85, ll. 523–28)

Unable to countenance so terrible a waste of beauty and passion, and loath to lose yet one more opportunity to indulge himself in an orgy of sensual rapture, the young Wilde translates Charmides and the white girl to Hades where in death's despite and through the good offices of Venus, they are brought together in an intensely erotic union of "rapturous bliss" (89, l. 633).

The pattern one discerns in "Charmides"—an act of daring, the product of both curiosity and desire, which incurs the wrath of the gods—as well as the type—that is, what I term the Charmides Self—are basic to some of Wilde's most famous works, including *The Picture of Dorian Gray*. Those familiar with the novel will recognize this Wildean type in the book's handsome and daring hero. But Lord Henry Wotton and Basil Hallward also are projections of this type. In other words, the three central characters of the novel in their own several ways mirror Wilde's pagan self.[8] Briefly stated, Dorian is the Charmides Self as romance hero, the quester seeking adventure in the magical realm of sensations; Basil is the Charmides Self as artist; whereas Lord Henry is the Charmides Self in its ultimate stage: the Charmides Self as philosopher and mentor.

Dorian as Charmides Self can best be seen in terms of the romance tradition, that is, as a young knight who sets out upon a quest in the course of which he has many adventures. Viewing Dorian, thus, in no way violates the nature of Wilde's fiction, which itself can best be understood in terms of narrative romance and what Robert Kiely calls the English romantic novel.[10]

Wilde was contemptuous of the naturalistic novelist of the day—Emile Zola bearing the brunt of his criticism. For instance, in "The Decay of Lying," Vivian, in the course of his dialogue with Cyril, finds Zola's work

> entirely wrong from beginning to end, and wrong not on the ground of morals, but on the ground of art. From any ethical standpoint it is just what it should be. The author is perfectly truthful, and describes things exactly as they happen. . . . But from the standpoint of art, what can be said in favour of the author of *L'Assommoir*, *Nana*, and *Pot-Bouille*? Nothing. Mr. Ruskin once described the characters in George Eliot's novels as being like the sweepings of a Pentonville omnibus, but M. Zola's characters are much worse. They have their dreary vices, and their drearier virtues. The record of their lives is absolutely without interest. Who cares what happens to them? In literature we require distinction, charm, beauty and imaginative power.[11]

"Imaginative power," that, in Vivian's opinion—as well as in Wilde's—is what was lacking in the naturalistic novel. Speaking of Balzac, Wilde's favorite novelist, as being "a most remarkable combination of the artistic temperament with the scientific spirit," Vivian points out to Cyril that the difference between a Zola novel and a Balzac novel "is the difference between unimaginative realism and imaginative reality."[12] Opposed to the basic principle of the traditional novel, that is, the mimetic principle, Wilde sought in *Dorian Gray* to write fiction which would be the product of "imaginative reality," one which would embody the artist's own subjective impressions of life. As Epifanio San Juan has said, "the function of mirroring reality serves less an imitative than an idealizing purpose" in Wilde's work where "the dimensions of reality reach us only after their passage, in sensory experience, through the peculiarly tuned sensibility of an individual."[13]

This rather Paterian view of art makes Wilde highly susceptible to the strengths and special appeal of romance. And, as we have seen, in his early sonnet, "Hélas!," Wilde, at the outset of his artistic career, connected the quest for beauty with romance. Moreover, Dorian, at the height of his adventures, explicitly links "his search for sensations that would be at once new and delightful" with "that element of strangeness that is so essential to romance" (132). Even after his gruesome experience in Reading Gaol, could Wilde ever have penned a novel in what he viewed as the realistic tradition of his day or have written *Dorian Gray* under the impression that he must not intrude such elements as a Faustian pact with the Devil and the magic of an aging portrait?

If, then, *The Picture of Dorian Gray* is in some important respects more romance than novel, its hero is more knight than knave. Dorian, unlike so many of his contemporaries in the realistic novel of the day, is an aristocrat whose business is not to do so bourgeois a thing as to make money, but, rather, to devote himself to the higher spheres of conduct. Initially the protégé of Lord Henry Wotton's aunt, Lady Agatha, who has called him to good works among the poor in the East End of London, Dorian is, in the opening scene of the novel, about to attend to yet a higher calling, one which comes to him with the impact and the effect of an epiphany.

Having just responded with great emotion to Lord Henry's "strange panegyric on youth, his terrible warning of its brevity" (25), Dorian, "as if awakened from some dream" (24) gazes for the first time on the full-length portrait of himself just completed by his artist friend, Basil Hallward.

> When he saw it he drew back, and his cheeks flushed for a moment with pleasure. A look of joy came into his eyes, as if he had recognized himself for the first time. He stood there motionless and in wonder, dimly conscious that Hallward was speaking to him, but not catching the meaning of his words. The sense of his own beauty came on him like a revelation. He had never felt it before. (24–25)

Like the knights of old struck dumb by the vision of their goal, the Holy Grail, Dorian stands narcissus-like "gazing at the shadow of his own loveliness" (25) with Lord Henry's exhortation ringing in his ears:

> Ah! Realize your youth while you have it. Don't squander the gold of your days, listening to the tedious, trying to improve the hopeless failure, or giving away your life to the ignorant, the common, and the vulgar. These are the sickly aims, the false ideals, of our age. Live! Live the wonderful life that is in you! Let nothing be lost upon you. Be always searching for new sensations. Be afraid of nothing. . . . A new Hedonism—that is what our century wants. You might be its visible symbol. (22)

Inspired now to become, indeed, that "visible symbol" of a new way of life, Dorian daringly barters his soul away for eternal youth and beauty. Determined to sacrifice all for beauty and the life of the senses, he enlists under the banner of the new Hedonism which Lord Henry has prophesied and sets out to save his world "from that harsh, uncomely puritanism that," as he later views it, "is having, in our own day, its curious revival" (130).[14]

Filled "with a wild desire to know everything about life" (47), Dorian at first tentatively ventures forth into Piccadilly where for days he seeks to satisfy his curiosity by examining the faces he meets there, some fascinating, others fearful. But at length he determines "to go out in search of some adventure," recalling what Lord Henry had said "about the search for beauty being the real secret of life" (48). Consequently, one evening he finds himself wandering "eastward" where soon after he loses his "way in a labyrinth of grimy streets and black, grassless squares" (48).

Having descended into the demonic realm of London's East End, not as Lady Agatha's Christian knight, but as Lord Henry's quester in search of sensational adventures, Dorian, instead of seeking out the poor in the workhouses and hospitals, looks for beauty and pleasure and finds it in what he later describes as "an absurd little theatre, with great flaring gas-jets and gaudy play-bills" (48). "A hideous Jew," which he later characterizes as "such a monster," is the novel's counterpart to the demonic tempters of romance who seek to waylay the hero and divert him from his quest. And that Dorian's Jew, who entices him "with an air of gorgeous servility" (48) into the wretched theater, plays such a role is borne out by the fact that Sibyl Vane, the idyllically beautiful young actress Dorian discovers there, is, in the end, ironically, a temptress who draws our hero into the bourgeois morass of "real life" with its middle-class domesticities and philistine views and virtues.

Sibyl, despite her alluring profession, is a denizen of her demonic surroundings (the Wildean counterpart to the naturalistic novel's realistic settings), and in time, like Cinderella at the ball, she must return to her rags and ashes. Armed as he is with the twin charms of beauty and youth, Sibyl's hold over Dorian is temporary and ultimately serves but to promote his self-realization through the pursuit of beauty.

With the help of Lord Henry's timely disquisition on art and life designed to comfort Dorian on hearing of the actress's suicide, Dorian is able to accept Sibyl as "a wonderful tragic figure sent on to the world's stage to show the supreme reality of love" (105). For Dorian the whole episode has been, as he tells Lord Henry, "a marvelous experience. That is all. I wonder if life has still in store for me anything as marvelous" (103).

Marvelous, indeed, are to be his further adventures as he is led on (in Huysmansesque fashion)" to one form of beauty after another—exotic perfumes, strange and bizarre sorts of music, treasure troves of jewels, mysterious sins, and wild sensations—by his seemingly insatiable curiosity and desire for adventure. None, however, is more unexpected and grotesque than Dorian's final interview with Basil Hallward which ends with the murder of the painter. On this particular occasion, Basil has sought out Dorian in order to confront him with the ugly rumors centering about his name which have been circulating for some time throughout society. Desirous of being assured by Dorian that there is no truth in them, Basil presses his friend: "Deny them, Dorian, deny them! Can't you see what I am going through? My God! Don't tell me that you are bad, and corrupt, and shameful" (154). Enraged, Dorian escorts Basil to the attic schoolroom where after unveiling the portrait in all its hideous corruption, he fatally stabs him.

Basil's death at the hands of Dorian is, in a sense, a fitting climax to the relationship between the two men. For Basil's denial of his Charmides Self in Dorian has led not only to their estrangement, but also has effectually put an end to Basil's new artistic mode which, of course, culminated years earlier in his painting of Dorian's portrait. Under the dominance of Dorian's Charmides Self, Basil had developed his art in a new direction. "His personality," he once told Lord Henry,

> has suggested to me an entirely new manner in art, an entirely new mode of style. I see things differently, I think of them differently. I can now recreate life in a way that was hidden from me before. . . . Unconsciously he defines for me the lines of a fresh school, a school that is to have in it all the passion of the romantic spirit, all the perfection of the spirit that is Greek. (10)

That the ultimate expression of this new mode is the picture of Dorian is, of course, agreed by all. Yet Basil's response to his *chef-d'oeuvre* is ambivalent. On completing it, he announces to the surprise of Lord Henry and Dorian that he intends not to exhibit it before the public, because, as he says, "I am afraid that I have shown in it the secret of my own soul" (5). Continuing, then, with a statement which seems to approve such an expression of the artist's self in his work, Basil explains to Lord Henry: "every portrait that is painted with feeling is a portrait of the artist, not the sitter" (5)—a view, one assumes, which is in keeping with his new artistic mode.

However, as the painter continues to talk, he appears to revert to old principles when he suddenly lashes out against those who "treat art as if it were meant to be a form of autobiography" (11). Making an assertion which is at odds with his earlier statement, Basil declares that "an artist should create beautiful things, but should put nothing of his own life into them. . . . We have lost the abstract sense of beauty. Some day I will show the world what it is; and for *that reason* the world shall never see my portrait of Dorian Gray" (11, emphasis added).

Although Basil's restatement of his reason for hiding the portrait is different in its emphasis from his initial statement, the reader is aware that the painter's resolve to keep the portrait from the prying eye of the public is motivated by personal rather than aesthetic considerations. In other words, Basil recognizes that in his portrait of Dorian, he has revealed his most carefully guarded secret, namely, his Charmides Self.

That what Lord Henry refers to as Basil's rather dull, conventional, intellectual self is but a mask for the Charmides Self is hinted at when, in introducing the reader to Basil, the narrator refers to the painter's "sudden disappearance some years ago," which had, at the time, caused considerable "public excitement, and [had given] rise to so many strange conjectures" (1). Moreover, Basil's initial conversation with Lord Henry about the identity of Dorian Gray reveals some curious facts, not the least of which is the painter's penchant for secrecy and mystery. "When I like people immensely," he explains, "I never tell their names to any one. It is like surrendering a part of them. I have grown to love secrecy." And as he goes on to remark, "when I leave town now I never tell my people where I am going. If I did, I would lose all my pleasure. It is a silly habit, I dare say, but somehow it seems to bring a great deal of romance into one's life" (4). One has the unmistakable feeling that the conventional, socially correct Basil is something of a "Bunburyist," one who, indeed, has something to hide, an aspect of himself which is deeply repressed.

However, as we come to know, this secret self suddenly has surfaced in the person of Dorian Gray, an occurrence that, at least initially, has had the effect of a traumatic shock on the artist. In language highly suggestive of one's encounter with another aspect of the self, Basil recalls for Lord Henry his first meeting with Dorian at Lady Brandon's "crush":

> I suddenly became conscious that some one was looking at me. I turned half-way round, and saw Dorian Gray for the first time. When our eyes met, I felt that I was growing pale. A curious sensation of terror came over me. I knew that I had come face to face with some one whose mere personality was so fascinating that, if I allowed it to do so, it would absorb my whole nature, my whole soul, my very art itself. (6)

So repressed has been his Charmides Self until the advent of Dorian in his life, that not even so astute and clever an observer of character as Lord Henry has fathomed in this outwardly rather dull, intellectual friend such another self. Having immediately recognized the portrait of Dorian Gray as a type of the Charmides Self—"Why, my dear Basil, he is a Narcissus" (11)—Lord Henry is quite surprised when Basil states: "I have put too much of myself into it" (2–3).

Basil's continued resolve to hide his Charmides Self (even though this strange cat is now, in a manner of speaking, out of the bag) is motivated by the artist's realization that not only has the influence of his Charmides Self been manifested in a new mode of art, but also in his idolatrous worship of physical beauty centered in Dorian, and in the painter's narcissistic self-love, projected in terms of a homosexual passion for Dorian—behavior not to be tolerated either by his puritanical conscience or his Hebraic, paternalistic society.

Consequently, Basil persuades himself that what he really sees and worships in Dorian is not the Charmides Self, but an ideal embodiment of beauty and goodness, a quintessential expression of the highly acceptable Ruskinian philosophy of art. Having convinced himself that the portrait is, indeed, a mirror image of the sitter's innocence and purity, Basil announces to Dorian his plan to exhibit the portrait in Paris. But by this time, the Charmides Self has taken on the corrupt and demonic expression the puritanical conscience habitually assigns it. Consequently, Basil could not have persisted in the folly of perpetuating his illusion if Dorian had allowed him to view it. As we know, Dorian does refuse his friend's request, even though he suspects, as well he should, that an intimate link exists between Basil's secret and his own.

Shunned by Dorian and unable to see his portrait, Basil becomes the hero's chief antagonist as he intensifies his moral crusade against his own and Dorian's Charmides Self which, as it rightly should, infuriates the youth and leads ultimately to the murder. Functioning in the end—to some extent at least—as a Fury harassing Dorian with moralistic preachments and dire warnings of impending doom, Basil is succeeded in his role by Jim Vane, Sibyl's vengeful brother, who after the artist's death, continues doggedly to haunt the hero's quest for sensations. Also an embodiment of Old Testament Law—the Hebraic code of "an eye for an eye"—Jim in his pursuit of Dorian, ironically, falls, himself, victim to a hunter's bullet.

Yet another example of Dorian's "charmed" life, Vane's fortuitous removal from the scene points up the fact that Dorian is, in the end, self-defeated, doomed by the enemy within, his own conscience. As his quest to become the "visible symbol" of a new hedonism draws to its close, Dorian, viewed from outside, appears to have attained his goal. Sinking deeply into old age, Lord Henry views his disciple as a miraculous being, who, having succeeded in his adventures, has returned with the talisman of perpetual youth and beauty with which he will bestow boons on his fellow beings. "Ah, Dorian, how happy you are!" he exclaims.

What an exquisite life you have had! You have drunk deeply of everything. You have crushed the grapes against your palate. Nothing has been hidden from you. And it has all been to you no more than the sound of music. It has not marred you. You are still the same. (216)

And although Dorian protests he is not the same, Lord Henry persists: "yes, you are the same. I wonder what the rest of your life will be. Don't spoil it by renunciations. At present you are a perfect type" (216).

Having succeeded in making art of his life, Dorian is, in Lord Henry's opinion, what the world needs: "You are the type of what the age is searching for" (217). Expressing his admiration for his pupil in terms especially dear to his own heart, Lord Henry continues: "I am so glad that you have never done anything, never carved a statue, or painted a picture, or produced anything outside yourself. Life has been your art. You have set yourself to music. Your days are your sonnets" (217).

Unfortunately, since Dorian can never grow older, never, in other words, move beyond the youthful stage to the fully matured, passive, philosophical stage of the Charmides Self which his mentor has attained, he, ironically, cannot share Lord Henry's ultimate philosophical point of view, that of a contemplative observer of culture who lives in the light of Pater's memorable aesthetic put forward in his early essay on Wordsworth. Lord Henry has long since learned not only to "treat life in the spirit of art,"[16] but also to cultivate highly refined states of mental activity—Pater's "impassioned contemplation"[17]—as ends in themselves.

Vampirelike, he has lived life intensely but at a distance through Dorian whose active pursuit of experience has been a source of great interest and pleasure to him. For instance, confronted with the fact of Dorian's infatuation with Sibyl, Lord Henry had been able to contemplate the affair without "the slightest pang of annoyance or jealousy." Rather, as the narrator tells us,

he was pleased by it. It made him [Dorian] a more interesting study. He had been always enthralled by the methods of natural science, but the ordinary subject-matter of that science had seemed to him trivial and of no import. And so he had begun by vivisecting himself, as he had ended by vivisecting others. (56)

Unable to mature into the passive philosophical observer of life, Dorian is overwhelmed at last by *ennui* as his adventures begin to cloy. Above all, he begins to moralize and, worse still, to talk about being good. And although Lord Henry begs him not to spoil it all "by renunciations" (216), his influence with Dorian is at an end. Now at the mercy of his conscience, the protagonist in the final phase of the novel is close to succumbing to the enemy, going so far as to consider his release of the country maid, Hetty, as an act of self-abnegation.[18] Of course, Lord Henry sees this act for what it really is—"I should think the novelty of the emotion must have given you a thrill of real pleasure"—but Dorian persists in his illusion:

> "Harry, you are horrible! You mustn't say these dreadful things. Hetty's heart is not broken. Of course she cried, and all that. But there is no disgrace upon her. She can live, like Perdita, in her garden of mint and marigolds." (210)

Increasingly haunted by a sense of doom, on the last evening of his life, Dorian returns home, his mind the prey of truly Hebraic thoughts: "There was purification in punishment," he mused to himself. "Not 'Forgive us our sins,' but 'Smite us for iniquities,' should be the prayer of man to a most just God" (220). Seeking some sign that his resolution to be good has registered its effect on his portrait, Dorian climbs the steps to the attic schoolroom where, to his dismay, he looks upon an even more corrupted image than before.

In what proves to be a final and climactic confrontation between protagonist and antagonist, Dorian, gazing with loathing on the conscience-corrupted portrait, now, in a supreme moment of illumination, sees it for what it really is: conscience. "It had been like conscience to him. Yes, it had been conscience." Convulsed with rage toward what is now clearly seen to be his tormentor, Dorian resolves to destroy it.

> He looked round, and saw the knife that had stabbed Basil Hallward. He had cleaned it many times, till there was no stain left upon it. It was bright, and glistened. As it had killed the painter, so it would kill *the painter's work, and all that that meant.* It would kill the past, and when that was dead he would be free. It would kill this monstrous soul-life, and, without its hideous warnings, he would be at peace. He seized the thing, and stabbed the picture with it. (223, emphasis added)

Having destroyed conscience—the enemy, within—Dorian through death is apotheosized in the redeemed portrait as the "visible symbol" of a new hedonism—an entirely appropriate conclusion to a hedonist romancer's quest.

That Wilde in seeking to blunt what Isobel Murray characterizes as the "hysterical" criticism of the first version of his novel[19] which had appeared in the pages of *Lippincott's Monthly Magazine* in 1890, sought to cast his conclusion in a morally acceptable light, may be inferred from the fact that he insisted to the newspapers that his novel, indeed, had what he called a "terrible moral": "All excess," he wrote in a letter to the *St. James Gazette*, "as well as all renunciation, brings its own punishment." Basil, he observed, is punished for "worshipping physical beauty far too much"; Dorian is punished for "having led a life of mere sensation and pleasure"; and Lord Henry is punished for being "merely the spectator of life."[20] Yet the resolution of the plot, as I read it, which belies this stated view, is more in keeping with Wilde's behavior toward earlier embodiments of the Charmides Self. For instance, as one will recall, he mitigated the rather harsh punishment the gods had meted out to Charmides; and in his short story, "Lord Arthur Savile's Crime," he had entirely absolved his handsome young hero who, having murdered the fat, ugly little cheiromantist Septimus Podgers, marries Sybil and flies to an idyllic country house where he leads an untroubled, guilt-free life of pagan bliss. "For them," the narrator tells us, "romance was not killed by reality. They always felt young."

Was the author of *Dorian Gray*, increasingly uneasy about the way in which his heroes invariably were extricated from their sinful pasts, and facing an increasingly hostile press and public, willing to allow romance to be killed by reality—a principle he habitually associated with the Hebraic spirit which plagued Victorian England and which begat the naturalistic novel? Perhaps so. But, in the spirit of romance, I prefer to believe that, in the end, an indulgent, albeit ironic Oscar, was moved to compose a denouement which would enable us (as well as himself) to have it both ways.

Notes

1. I Samuel 14: 24, 27, 43, King James Bible.

2. *The Renaissance*, ed. Donald Hill (Berkeley: University of California Press, 1980), 177.

3. Oscar Wilde, *Poems and Poems in Prose*, vol. 1, ed. Bobby Fong and Karl Beckson, *Complete Works of Oscar Wilde*, ed. Russell Jackson and Ian Small (Oxford: Oxford University Press, 2000), 157, ll. 12–14. All further references to the poetry are to this edition and cited in the text.

4. I use the phrase "Hebraic spirit" and the term "Hebraism" throughout as Matthew Arnold defined them in his essay, "Hebraism and Hellenism" in his *Culture and Anarchy*. Wilde was entirely familiar with Arnold's use of these terms.

5. Richard Ellmann in "Overtures to *Salome*" in *Oscar Wilde: A Collection of Critical Essays*, ed. by Ellmann (Englewood Cliffs, N.J.: Prentice-Hall, 1969), 86, discusses Wilde's struggle in terms of Pater vs. Ruskin: "they came to stand heraldically, burning unicorn and uninflamed satyr, in front of two portals of his mental theatre. He sometimes allowed them to battle, at other times tried to reconcile them." Jan B. Gordon sees it in terms of Arnold's Hebraism and Hellenism in "Hebraism and Hellenism, and *The Picture of Dorian Gray*," *Victorian Newsletter*, no. 33 (spring 1968), 36–38.

6. Hesketh Pearson, *Oscar Wilde* (New York and London: Harper, 1946), 34.

7. Wilde's new Helen was the celebrated actress Lillie Langtry.

8. *The Picture of Dorian Gray*, The World's Classics ed., ed. Isobel Murray (Oxford and New York: Oxford University Press, 1981), 15. All further references to the novel are to this edition and cited in the text.

9. As Wilde once admitted, "it [that strange coloured book of mine] contains much of me in it. Basil Hallward is what I think I am: Lord Henry what the world thinks me: Dorian what I would like to be—in other ages, perhaps." *The Letters of Oscar Wilde*, ed. Rupert Hart-Davis (New York: Harcourt, Brace & World, 1962), 352.

10. Kiely's remarks throughout his introduction to *The Romantic Novel in England* (Cambridge: Harvard University Press, 1972), in particular, those concerning the relationship of the romance tradition to the English romantic novel are applicable to much that Wilde is doing in *Dorian Gray*.

11. "The Decay of Lying," in *Oscar Wilde, Selected Writings*, ed. Richard Ellmann (London: Oxford University Press, 1961), 8.

12. *Selected Writings*, 10–11.

13. *The Art of Oscar Wilde* (Princeton: Princeton University Press, 1967), 33–34.

14. Ellmann in "Overtures" (88), believes the "curious revival" of puritanism to have been associated in Wilde's mind with Ruskin.

15. These bizarre adventures are clearly the result of Dorian's fascinated reading of "the yellow book that Lord Henry had sent him," (125) usually assumed by readers to be J.-K. Huysmans's notorious novel, *A Rebours*.

16. "Wordsworth" in *Selected Writings of Walter Pater*, ed. Harold Bloom (New York: New American Library, 1974), 139.

17. Ibid., 137.

18. If it is possible to read Wilde's novel in terms of the internalized quest which critics have associated with such works of the High Romantics as Blake's *Jerusalem* and Wordsworth's *The Prelude*, Dorian's adventures as Charmides Self represent what Harold Bloom calls Prometheus (i.e., the first phase of the total quest which concerns, in part, in Bloom's words, "the libido's struggle against repressiveness." Although Dorian does, especially in his relations with Hetty, make an effort toward transcending or annihilating Selfhood (Blake's Spectre of Urthona), he does not make a serious and sustained effort toward the goal of the second phase or "the Real Man." See Bloom, "The Internalization of Quest Romance," in *The Ringers in the Tower* (Chicago: University of Chicago Press, 1971), 21–22.

19. Introduction to *The Picture of Dorian Gray*, vii.

20. Letter to the editor of the *St. James Gazette*, 26 June 1890 in *Letters of Oscar Wilde*, 258.

Chronology

1854	Born in Dublin on October 16 to Protestant parents: William Wilde, a distinguished oculist, and Jane Elgee Wilde, a writer (using the pseudonym Speranze).
1864–71	Educated at Portora Royal School, Enniskillen.
1871–74	Studies classics at Trinity College, Dublin.
1874–78	Studies at Magdalen College, Oxford, where his professors include Walter Pater. Wins the Newdigate Prize for poetry and receives a B.A. in greats (classics) with first class honours.
1876	Father dies.
1879	Moves to London.
1881	Publishes *Poems*. Writes *Vera; or the Nihilists* (first produced in New York in 1883).
1881–82	Lectures in the United States and Canada on the aesthetic movement.
1883	Writes *The Duchess of Padua* (first produced in New York under the title *Guido Ferranti* in 1891).
1884	Marries Constance Lloyd, a family friend from Dublin.
1885	Son Cyril born.
1886	Son Vyvyan born.

1887–89	Editor of *Woman's World*.
1888	Publishes *The Happy Prince and Other Tales*.
1889	Publishes "The Portrait of Mr. W. H." in *Blackwood's Magazine*.
1890	Publishes "The Picture of Dorian Gray" in *Lippincott's Magazine*.
1891	Publishes "The Soul of Man under Socialism" in *Fortnightly Magazine*, *Intentions*, *The Picture of Dorian Gray* in book form, *Lord Arthur Savile's Crime and Other Stories*, and *A House of Pomegranates*. Writes *Salomé* in Paris. Meets Lord Alfred Douglas.
1892	*Lady Windermere's Fan* produced. *Salomé* banned by the Lord Chamberlain. Publishes limited edition of *Poems*.
1893	*A Woman of No Importance* produced; *Salomé* published in French. *Lady Windermere's Fan* published.
1894	*Salomé* published in English with illustrations by Aubrey Beardsley. *The Sphinx* and *A Woman of No Importance* published.
1895	*An Ideal Husband* and *The Importance of Being Earnest* produced. Wilde sues for libel Douglas's father, the Marquess of Queensberry, who has objected to Wilde's relationship with his son. Queensberry acquitted. Wilde arrested the same day for sexual offences; after a first trial results in a hung jury, he is convicted at a second trial and sentenced to two years' hard labor.
1895–97	Imprisoned at Reading.
1896	Mother dies.
1897	Writes letter to Lord Alfred Douglas that will be published (in edited form) as *De Profundis* (finally published complete in 1962). On release from prison, Wilde goes to France, Italy and Switzerland and lives abroad until his death.
1898	Publishes *The Ballad of Reading Gaol*. Constance Wilde dies.
1899	Publishes *The Importance of Being Earnest* and *An Ideal Husband*.
1900	On November 30, dies in Paris, where he is buried.

Contributors

HAROLD BLOOM is Sterling Professor of the Humanities at Yale University. Educated at Cornell and Yale universities, he is the author of more than 30 books, including *Shelley's Mythmaking* (1959), *The Visionary Company* (1961), *Blake's Apocalypse* (1963), *Yeats* (1970), *The Anxiety of Influence* (1973), *A Map of Misreading* (1975), *Kabbalah and Criticism* (1975), *Agon: Toward a Theory of Revisionism* (1982), *The American Religion* (1992), *The Western Canon* (1994), *Omens of Millennium: The Gnosis of Angels, Dreams, and Resurrection* (1996), *Shakespeare: The Invention of the Human* (1998), *How to Read and Why* (2000), *Genius: A Mosaic of One Hundred Exemplary Creative Minds* (2002), *Hamlet: Poem Unlimited* (2003), *Where Shall Wisdom Be Found?* (2004), and *Jesus and Yahweh: The Names Divine* (2005). In addition, he is the author of hundreds of articles, reviews, and editorial introductions. In 1999, Professor Bloom received the American Academy of Arts and Letters' Gold Medal for Criticism. He has also received the International Prize of Catalonia, the Alfonso Reyes Prize of Mexico, and the Hans Christian Andersen Bicentennial Prize of Denmark.

RICHARD ELLMANN was a professor at Emory University. He published numerous works and is best known for his literary biographies, including those covering Wilde, Yeats, and Joyce. Some of his other texts include the anthology *The Modern Tradition* and *The Norton Anthology of Modern and Contemporary Poetry*, both of which he co-edited.

GUY WILLOUGHBY was a senior lecturer at the University of Pretoria. In addition to his book on Wilde, his other work concerning Wilde includes a serialized radio play of *The Picture of Dorian Gray*. Guy Willougby was also an actor, playwright, novelist, and journalist.

RONALD KNOWLES has been a senior lecturer in English literature at the University of Reading. He has published books on Shakespeare, Pinter, and Swift and also is the editor of *King Henry VI Part 2* in the Arden Shakespeare series.

MICHAEL PATRICK GILLESPIE is a professor of English and graduate director at Marquette University. His work includes editing Norton's editions of *The Importance of Being Earnest* and *The Picture of Dorian Gray*; he also has written on *The Picture of Dorian Gray* for Twayne's Masterwork Studies series.

JOHN PAUL RIQUELME is a professor of English at Boston University. He is the author of *Gothic and Modernism* and also has written on *Tess of the D'Urbervilles*, *Dracula*, and T. S. Eliot and romanticism.

CHRISTOPHER S. NASSAAR is a senior lecturer at the American University of Beirut. He is the author of a critical study of Wilde, *Into the Demon Universe*; a study guide of *The Importance of Being Earnest*; and of many other articles and notes. He also has published *Earnest Revisited: A Novel* and is in the midst of completing *The Resurrection of Dorian Gray: A Sequel*.

BURKHARD NIEDERHOFF is chair of English literature at Ruhr-Universität Bochum. He has published texts on Robert Louis Stevenson and on English comedy.

JAMES G. NELSON is a professor emeritus at the University of Wisconsin in Madison. He is the author of *The Sublime Puritan: Milton and the Victorians*, as well as of a trilogy of books on publishing in the 1890s in England.

Bibliography

Ackroyd, Peter. *The Last Testament of Oscar Wilde*. London: Hamish Hamilton, 1983.

Anger, Suzy. *Victorian Interpretation*. Ithaca, N.Y.: Cornell University Press, 2005.

Bashford, Bruce. *OscarWilde: The Critic as Humanist*. Madison [N.J.]: Fairleigh Dickinson University Press; London: Associated University Presses, 1999.

Beckson, Karl. *The Religion of Art: A Modernist Theme in British Literature, 1885–1925*. Brooklyn: AMS, 2006.

Bristow, Joseph, ed. *Oscar Wilde and Modern Culture: The Making of a Legend*. Athens: Ohio University Press, 2008.

———. *Wilde Writings: Contextual Conditions*. Toronto: University of Toronto Press in association with the UCLA Center for Seventeenth- and Eighteenth-Century Studies and the William Andrews Clark Memorial Library, 2003.

Brown, Julia Prewitt. *Cosmopolitan Criticism: Oscar Wilde's Philosophy of Art*. Charlottesville: University Press of Virginia, 1997.

Budziak, Anna. *Text, Body and Indeterminacy: Doppelganger Selves in Pater and Wilde*. Newcastle upon Tyne, England: Cambridge Scholars, 2008.

Burt, E. S. *Regard for the Other: Autothanatography in Rousseau, De Quincey, Baudelaire, and Wilde*. New York: Fordham University Press, 2009.

Carroll, Joseph. "Aestheticism, Homoeroticism, and Christian Guilt in *The Picture of Dorian Gray*." *Philosophy and Literature* 29, no. 2 (October 2005): 286–304.

Castle, Gregory. "Bildung and the 'Bonds of Dominion': Wilde and Joyce." In *Reading the Modernist Bildungsroman*. Gainesville: University Press of Florida, 2006.

Coakley, Davis. *Oscar Wilde, the Importance of Being Irish*. Dublin: Town House, 1994.

145

Corballis, Richard, and Julie A. Hibbard, ed. *The Importance of Reinventing Oscar: Versions of Wilde During the Last 100 Years*. Amsterdam, Netherlands: Rodopi, 2002.

Craft, Christopher. "Come See about Me: Enchantment of the Double in *The Picture of Dorian Gray*."*Representations* 91 (Summer 2005): 109–36.

Dawson, Terence. *The Effective Protagonist in the Nineteenth-Century British Novel: Scott, Brontë, Eliot, Wilde*. Aldershot, Hampshire, England; Burlington, Vt.: Ashgate, 2004.

Downey, Katherine Brown. *Perverse Midrash: Oscar Wilde, Andrè Gide, and Censorship of Biblical Drama*. New York: Continuum, 2004.

Ellmann, Richard. *Oscar Wilde*. New York: Knopf, distributed by Random House, 1988.

Eltis. Sos. *Revising Wilde: Society and Subversion in the Plays of Oscar Wilde*. Oxford; New York: Clarendon Press, 1996.

Frankel, Nicholas. *Oscar Wilde's Decorated Books*. Ann Arbor: University of Michigan Press, 2000.

Gagnier, Regenia A. *Idylls of the Marketplace: Oscar Wilde and the Victorian Public*. Stanford, Calif.: Stanford University Press, 1986.

Guy, Josephine. *Studying Oscar Wilde: History, Criticism, and Myth*. Greensboro, N.C.: ELT, 2006.

Halpern, Richard. *Shakespeare's Perfume: Sodomy and Sublimity in the Sonnets, Wilde, Freud, and Lacan*. Philadelphia: University of Pennsylvania Press, 2002.

Hofer, Matthew, and Gary Scharnhorst, eds. Oscar *Wilde in America: The Interviews*. Urbana: University of Illinois Press, 2010.

Horan, Patrick M. *The Importance of Being Paradoxical: Maternal Presence in the Works of Oscar Wilde*. Madison, N.J.: Fairleigh Dickinson University Press; London; Cranbury, N.J.: Associated University Presses, 1997.

Ivory, Yvonne. "Wilde's Renaissance: Poison, Passion, and Personality." *Victorian Literature and Culture* 35, no. 2 (2007): 517–36.

Keane, Robert N., ed. *Oscar Wilde: The Man, His Writings, and His World*. New York: AMS Press, 2003.

Killeen, Jarlath. *The Fairy Tales of Oscar Wilde*. Aldershot, England; Burlington, Vt.: Ashgate, 2007.

Knox, Melissa. *Oscar Wilde in the 1990s: The Critic as Creator*. Rochester, N.Y.: Camden House, 2001.

Lalonde, Jeremy. "A 'Revolutionary Outrage': *The Importance of Being Earnest* as Social Criticism." *Modern Drama* 48, no. 4 (Winter 2005): 659–76.

Levy, Anita. *Reproductive Urges: Popular Novel-Reading, Sexuality, and the English Nation*. Philadelphia: University of Pennsylvania Press, 1999.

McCormack, Jerusha, ed. *Wilde the Irishman*. New Haven: Yale University Press, 1998.

Miller, J. Hillis. "Oscar in The Tragic Muse." *Arizona Quarterly: A Journal of American Literature, Culture, and Theory* 62, no. 3 (Autumn 2006): 31–44.

Miyata, Rinako. *Oscar Wilde and Class*. Portland, Ore.: Book East, 2007.

Nelson, Walter W. *Oscar Wilde from Ravenna to Salome: A Survey of Contemporary English Criticism*. Dublin: Dublin University Press, 1987.

O'Connor, Sean. *Straight Acting: Popular Gay Drama from Wilde to Rattigan*. London; Washington, D.C.: Cassell, 1998.

Roditi, Edouard. *Oscar Wilde*. New York: New Directions, 1986.

Sandulescu, George, ed. *Rediscovering Oscar Wilde*. Gerrards Cross: Colin Smythe, 1994.

Small, Ian. *Oscar Wilde Revalued: An Essay on New Materials &Methods of Research*. Greensboro, N.C.: ELT Press, 1993.

Smith, Timothy D'Arch. *Bunbury: Two Notes on Oscar Wilde*. Bicary, Broze, France: Winged Lion, 1998.

Summers, Claude J. *Gay Fictions: Wilde to Stonewall: Studies in a Male Homosexual Literary Tradition*. New York: Continuum, 1990.

Tufescu, Florina. *Oscar Wilde's Plagiarism: The Triumph of Art over Ego*. Dublin; Portland, Ore.: Irish Academic, 2008.

Upchurch, David A. *Wilde's Use of Irish Celtic Elements in The Picture of Dorian Gray*. New York: P. Lang, 1992.

The Wildean: Journal of the Oscar Wilde Society. London: Oscar Wilde Society.

Woodcock, George. *Oscar Wilde: The Double Image*. Montreal; New York: Black Rose Books, 1989.

Acknowledgments

Richard Ellmann, "The Uses of Decadence: Wilde, Yeats and Joyce." From *Literary Interrelations: Ireland, England and the World*, edited by Wolfgang Zach and Heinz Kosok. Copyright © 1987 by Gunter Narr Verlag Tübingen.

Guy Willoughby, "A Poetics for Living: Christ and the Meaning of Sorrow in *De Profundis*." From *Art and Christhood: The Aesthetics of Oscar Wilde*. Published by Fairleigh Dickinson University Press. Copyright © 1993 by Associated University Presses.

Ronald Knowles, "Bunburying with Bakhtin: A Carnivalesque Reading of *The Importance of Being Earnest*." From *Essays in Poetics* 20 (Autumn 1995): 170–81. Published by Keele University. Copyright © 1995 by Ronald Knowles.

Michael Patrick Gillespie, "The Victorian Impulse in Contemporary Audiences: The Regularization of *The Importance of Being Earnest*." From *Oscar Wilde and the Poetics of Ambiguity*. Copyright © 1996 by the Board of Regents of the State of Florida. Reprinted courtesy of the University Press of Florida.

John Paul Riquelme, "Oscar Wilde's Aesthetic Gothic: Walter Pater, Dark Enlightenment, and *The Picture of Dorian Gray*." From *Modern Fiction Studies* 46, no. 3 (Fall 2000): 609–31. Copyright © 2000 for the Purdue Research Foundation by the Johns Hopkins University Press.

Index